CLARENDON MEDIEVAL AND TUDOR SERIES

General Editor

J. A. W. BENNETT

CLARENDON MEDIEVAL AND TUDOR SERIES

MS. Bodley 294, f. 9

MS. Bodley 902, f. 8

AMANS AND GENIUS

SELECTIONS FROM
JOHN GOWER

With an Introduction, Notes, and
Glossary by
J. A. W. BENNETT

.

OXFORD
AT THE CLARENDON PRESS
1968

Oxford University Press, Ely House, London W. 1

GLASGOW NEW YORK TORONTO MELBOURNE WELLINGTON
CAPE TOWN SALISBURY IBADAN NAIROBI LUSAKA ADDIS ABABA
BOMBAY CALCUTTA MADRAS KARACHI LAHORE DACCA
KUALA LUMPUR HONG KONG TOKYO

PRINTED IN GREAT BRITAIN

CONTENTS

INTRODUCTION

IF Gower's name has any associations today for the generality of readers they are either with the Chorus of *Pericles* or with the Dedication of Chaucer's masterpiece. The former—in lamer verse than Gower himself was ever guilty of—suggests that Shakespeare thought the last and longest story in the *Confessio Amantis* worth his perusal. By directing the *Boke of Troilus* to 'moral Gower' Chaucer undesignedly fastened on his friend an epithet that has come to connote the conventional, the insipid, or the smug—whereas its original context implies a deep respect for Gower, as for the 'philosophical Strode' who is named in the same line, and who, no less seriously, was to hail Gower as a second Virgil, an 'Athlete of Song'.[1] There is little doubt that the works of Gower which Chaucer had in mind were the French *Mirour de l'omme* and the Latin *Vox Clamantis*—books which Gower's own Venus was to characterize as redolent of 'vertu moral' (*Confessio*, viii. 2925). On the same occasion the goddess greets Chaucer as 'mi disciple and mi poete'; and in the middle of the *Confessio* the lover depicts his mistress as eager 'To rede or here of Troilus'. The quiet obliqueness of the compliment is characteristic of Gower, and the line evokes the splendid miniature in which Chaucer himself is seen reading the poem to an aristocratic audience.[2] The taste reflected in that poem, and that miniature, is essentially the taste to which the *Confessio* appealed. Its whole system of amatory conceptions and usages—to use Huizinga's terms—was that current in the aristocratic conversation of the time. Puttenham properly described Gower as a Courtly Maker, and the many elegant manuscripts of his English poem—some illuminated by the brilliant court painter Herman Scheerre[3]—remind us that English taste in poetry, in painting, and

[1] See p. 123 below.
[2] MS. CCCC 61, frontispiece often reproduced (e.g. in G. M. Trevelyan, *Social History of England*, f.p.).
[3] See p. xxii. For Scheerre see Margaret Rickert, *Painting in Britain: the Middle Ages* (1954), pp. 181–4, etc.

in dress was never more refined and exquisite than in the age of
the Wilton Dyptich and the reign of Richard the Connoisseur,
Gower's patron, and the prime object of his moral exhortations.
In the poetry as in the art native and foreign influences were
subtly blended, to the increase rather than the loss of patriotism;
Gower's *amor patriae* is expressed in French—'O gentile Engle-
terre, a toi jescrits'—no less easily than in the Latin of

> Si tamen esse potest quod felix esset in orbe,
> Dudum felices nos dedit esse deus:[1]

It was still very much a courtly or well-to-do audience that
Caxton had in view when he chose the *Confessio* to follow hard
upon his print of the *Canterbury Tales*. If some dull English
writers and some better Scottish ones seem to pay Gower vague
lip-service only, this does not mean that he was more respected
than read. Dunbar's presentation of the Queen of Love in his
Golden Targe perhaps owes something to the closing scene in the
Confessio of the poet whose 'sugared lips' and 'aureate tongue' he
professedly admired. Gower was anthologized in the fifteenth
century as often as Chaucer, and indeed sometimes works by the
two poets are intermixed;[2] whilst a lyric of that century
charmingly catches the spirit of Gower's penitential dialogue:

> My gostly fadir, y me confesse
> First to God and then to yow,
> That at a wyndow—wot ye how?
> I stale a cosse of grete swetnes,
> Which don was out avysnes
> But hit is doon not undoon now. . . .[3]

Here is *courtoisie* in its most appealing, and most distinctively

[1] *Vox Clamantis*, ii. 17–18 (and ff.).

[2] e.g. the 'Findern MS.' described by R. H. Robbins, *PMLA*, lxix (1954), 610–
42), which includes parts of several of the extracts in the present volume, alongside
Chaucer's story of Thisbe from the *Legend of Good Women*, the *Complaint of Venus*,
etc. MS. Rawl. D82 (incl. *CA*, viii. 2377–970) was originally part of a large volume
of secular literature: see *Bodleian Library Record*, vii (1966), 234–41.

[3] The whole poem is accessible in Sidgwick and Jackson, *Early English Lyrics*
(1907), No. xvii. In *CA*, v. 6558 ff. Genius gently asks Amans if he has 'stolen eny
cuss', and he replies: 'My fader, nay, and that is routhe, For be mi will I *am* a thief'
(confessing to a sin of *intent*). [Cf. *The English Poems of Charles of Orleans*, ed.
R. Steele (1941), ll. 5275–9.]

English posture; and Gower's attraction lasted for just so long as this kind of language was the *koine* of English aristocratic society.

Yet to label him as 'typically medieval' is to be as unjust to the Middle Ages as to him, unless we allow that medieval refinement did not exclude natural impulses. In fact an awareness of these forces pervades every love-tale that Gower tells, and even determines his choice of such an *exemplum* as the story of Achilles and Deidamia:

> Wher Kinde wole himselve rihte
> After the philosphres sein,
> Ther mai no wiht be therayein:
> And that was thilke time seene.
> The longe nyhtes hem betuene
> Nature, which mai noght forbere,
> Hath mad hem bothe forto stere;
> Thei kessen ferst, and overmore
> The hihe weie of loves lore
> Thei gon, and al was don in dede,
> Wherof lost is the maydenhede;
>
> (*CA*, v. 3058–68)

For Gower, as for Chaucer, Kind—who sets in the beloved 'beaute with bounte' (v. 2595), virtue as well as comeliness—ranks above Venus. God himself, 'the hihe makere of natures' (vii. 1508; cf. v. 4918–19) has established that *lex naturae* which binds 'every lifissh creature' and of which sexual love is but a part. Conversely, 'unkindness' characterizes all the sins as Gower's priest describes them; Gower even invents 'unkinde-schipe' (matching his 'kindeschipe') to describe the Envy who

> Is of the courte the comun wenche
> And halt tavernes for to schenche
> That drink which makth the herte brenne
>
> (*CA*, ii. 3096–9; cf. *Inferno*, xiii. 64–66)

—a glimpse of the seamier side of palace life, confirming the view that 'the court to *some* doth profit And *some* ben evere in o plit' (v. 2251–2). Working to a firm scale of values, Gower had no difficulty in relating Nature to Grace on the one side and to *Courtoisie* on the other. Service in love 'to Kinde acordeth' but

> It is to Kinde no pleasaunce
> That man above his sustienaunce
> Unto the gold schal serve and bowe,
> For that may no reson avowe [justify] (*CA*, v. 121–4)

—Reason being his other touchstone. It is Reason that forbids
men 'mad lich to the godlihede' both to act like beasts and to
treat other men as beasts in the slaughter that is glorified as war.
For him Alexander is no more than the disturber of the world's
peace—and to no purpose:

> Lo now, for what profit
> Of werre it helpeth for to ryde
> For coveitise and worldes pride
> To sle the worldes men aboute,
> As bestes whiche gon theroute.
> For every lif which reson can
> Oghth wel to knowe that a man
> Ne scholde thorgh no tirannie
> Lich to these othre bestes die
> Til Kinde wolde for him sende. (iii. 2468–78)

So the church, mansoul, and 'the well of pity' are all defiled by
wars of conquest and crusade. The apparent irrelevance of such
censures to the lover's shrift bespeaks Gower's preoccupations.
This graceful poet of the court was as sensitive as Chaucer (and
Deschamps) to the horrors of 'contek, with blody knif . . .
outhees, and fiers outrage' that for the readers of the *Confessio* as
of the Knight's Tale were part of the unending war with France.
The moral concerns that persist, if sometimes only in the form
of a yearning for a golden age, in each of his major works, and
most markedly in the Prologue of the poem written at a king's
behest—these concerns are always expressed in terms of peace
and the 'common profit' in state and church:

> This clerk seith yee, that other nay,
> And thus thei dryve forth the day,
> And ech of hem himself amendeth
> Of worldes good, bot non entendeth
> To that which comun profit were. (*CA*, Prol. 373–8)

At times this concern may seem to be only a disguised yearning for good times gone. But more often it speaks in accents like those of the versatile and enlightened scientist-philosopher Nicholas Oresme, a mentor to the French king, who carried his belief in the common profit so far as to imperil princely prerogative in his *De Moneta*.

Gower's fondness for classical myth and story is a further reason for revising the general view of him as essentially medieval. It is not only that he is the first English transmitter of so many of the classical themes which Renaissance poets and painters were to embroider—giving us as he does not merely the common references to Helen and Dido, Phaeton and Pygmalion, Actaeon and Achilles, but the ampler tales of Ulysses, Penelope and Telegonus, Demetrius and Persius, Orestes and Diogenes; it is also that in his modest way he provided in the fifth book of his *Confessio* an English equivalent to Boccaccio's more elaborate *Genealogia Deorum*—a work likewise professedly undertaken by royal request. In that very book Boccaccio had remarked that in mythological learning the English were as yet *studiis tardi*; and Thomas Walsingham's *De generatione et natura deorum . . . cum interpretatione Ovidii* (post 1386), following belatedly on the activities of the English Friars resurrected by Miss Smalley,[1] is still apologetic in tone. But the Gower who presents Ovid without undue regard to the moralizing interpretations that festooned the medieval *Metamorphoses*, stands at no great distance in spirit from later humanists and translators. It is not surprising that Ben Jonson read widely in the *Confessio*, and—perhaps because he remembered Gower's own evocation of Ovid's *aurea prima aetas*[2] —introduced the poet into the masque *The Golden Age Restored*.

On the Continent the poetry of 'Venus, clerke Ovide' had long been a quarry for precepts and *exempla*: witness the encyclopedic Jean de Meun and amongst Gower's contemporaries Froissart, with whose verse Gower's has some affinities. The English poet doubtless took heed of these Ovidian allusions. But for him the

---

[1] See Beryl Smalley, *English Friars and Antiquity in the Early Fourteenth Century* (1960), *passim*.
[2] Cf. *CA*, v. 1–21 and *Vox Clamantis*, vi. 5–8 with *Metamorphoses*, l. 89 ff. Boccaccio has the same topic in *De Claris Mulieribus, ad init.* For Chaucer's treatment of it see J. N. Smith in *Medium Aevum*, xxxii (1963), 117.

Metamorphoses had a powerful direct appeal. It is the miraculous transformation of human lovers into bird, beast, or tree that most excites his sympathy and touches him to pity and to poetry. His very first tale (*CA*, i. 333) is of Diana and Actaeon—and it owes nothing to Froissart's flatter versions in *Le Joli Buisson de Jonece*, and in *L'Espinette amoureuse* (where it is confused with the tale of Cephalus and Procris). His renderings of the stories of Alcione and Philomela show how much more he was than a mere translator. It is Gower's Alcione, not Ovid's, who

> . . . fondeth in hire briddes forme
> If that sche mihte hirself conforme
> To do the plesance of a wif
> As sche dede in that other life.   (iv. 3109–12)

and the same fascination of mysterious physical change prompts him to pass from Benoit's Medea to Ovid's witchlike transformer of the aged Æson, and to linger (as many miniaturists of *Le Roman de la Rose* were to do) over Pygmalion's plight:

> He keste hire colde lippes ofte
> And wissheth that thei weren softe,
> And ofte he rouneth in hire ere,
> And ofte his arme now hier now there
> He leide, as he hir wolde embrace,
> And evere among he axeth grace,
> As thogh sche wiste what he mente.   (iv. 405–11)

More surprisingly, it allows him to include tales of incest and treat the victims with the gentleness due to those who were 'as who seith, enchanted'. Enchantment, too, adds glamour (in the stricter sense) to the ladies whom Rosiphelee sees riding on white horses through the forest-glade. Theirs is a *faye* beauty; hence they can disappear as silently and as suddenly as a cloud.

The magic, the mystery, and the morals of such tales may seem very 'unclassical', very un-Ovidian, and very far removed from the social themes of Gower's prologue and conclusion. But this is because we read the *Metamorphoses* in snatches at school and ignore its envelope: the opening narrative of creation and the golden age, the closing Pythagorean speculations and encomiums of Augustan peace, civic justice, and morality. Such topics would be as congenial as the tales themselves to the Gower who saw himself as a citizen of the New Troy, linked in its history and fortunes with Rome the Great. In this respect he is as 'Augustan' as the Dryden who shared his 'concernment' for Ovid's heroines (preferring them to Virgil's) and who so much admired the last book of Ovid's 'Fables'—and as the Addison who likewise translated and appraised parts of those stories.

The *Metamorphoses* was not the only work of Ovid familiar to the Middle Ages, or to Gower. From the *Heroides* he drew his versions of the story of Dido (iv. 80 ff.) and of Demophon and Phillis (iv. 731), not to mention incidental reminiscences; and behind his love-doctrine, as behind that of most medieval poets, lies the Ovid of the *Ars Amatoria*. Yet his presentation of *Amans*, the lover, is as distant from the cynicism of that work as it is from the naturalism of Jean de Meun's; and at one point in the *Vox Clamantis* he is at pains to dissociate himself from Ovid's counsel:

> Codice nempe suo referam que carmina vates
> Rettulit Ovidius, nec michi verba tenent. (v. 383–4)[1]

Amans certainly behaves for the most part according to the rules for a courtly lover that can be deduced from Andreas Capellanus. But the adulterous assumptions or intentions implicit in Andreas' book, as in many medieval love-songs or romances, are markedly absent. There is not even a hint that he is courting a married woman; and Genius his confessor goes out of his way to preach the virtues of the married state (see pp. 37–38), urging in the most matter-of-fact way that a maiden should be wedded

> Whyl sche the charge myhte bere
> Of children, which the world forbere
> Ne mai, bot if it scholde faile; (iv. 1495–7)

a very terse and orthodox counterpart to the discourse on plenitude on *Le Roman de la Rose*, which runs at full spate for a thousand lines. In the *Roman* Raison and Amors are at odds; in the *Confessio* Reason is a restraining rather than hostile force, warning against love's foolish excesses, or, in the words of a rubric for the

---

[1] The lines are intercalated amongst a series of adaptations of verses from *Ars Amatoria*. The number of lines borrowed from all of Ovid's works in *VC* is listed by Eric W. Stockton, *The Major Latin Works of John Gower* (Seattle, 1962), who specifies them in his notes.

eighteen balades which in some manuscripts follow the *Confessio*, '*la sotie* de cellui qui par amours aime par especial';[1] these balades themselves celebrating the loyalty of those who kept their marriage vows. The English Genius, again, as opposed to the priest of that name in the *Roman*, is a priest of Charite as much as of Amour: always ready to show, as in the tale of Constantine and Sylvester, 'How charite may helpe a man / To bothe worldes' (ii. 3498), and so preparing us for the final lesson of the poem.

All this chimes with Gower's censure elsewhere of *gallicum peccatum*, the vice of adulterous love new come in from France.[2] He shows us love in a cool English climate, different from the sultry Provence of the *Flamenca* or Boccaccio's Florence or Naples. *Amans*, devoted though he is, does not wholly conform to the stock figure of amorous devotion as found in Froissart's love-visions. Indeed, the verse is at its most vibrant when he flatly refuses to demonstrate his love in time-honoured fashion by going on crusade or *chivachie* (see p. 39 below).

The poet's first-hand knowledge of violence probably did not extend beyond the uprising that historians call the Peasants' Revolt which was at its bloodiest in Gower's Southwark and left an indelible mark on his Latin allegorical works of satire and chronicle. Nothing suggests that he himself ever followed the wars or even crossed the Channel. Yet the idioms and technical terms of shipmen and the sea are amongst the most distinctive features of his language. The very first, indeed the only, glimpse we have of him *in propria persona* is

> In Temse when it was flowende
> As I bi bote cam rowende. (prol. 39–40*; cf. p. 172 below)

[1] 'Sotie' and 'fol emprise' is equally the fault of the 'covetous' or 'newfangle' lover who finds something to please him in all women:

> Som on, for that she is camused,
> Som on, for that sche hath not ben used,
> Som on, for sche can daunce and singe,
> So that som thing to his likinge
> He fint. . . . (v. 2479 ff.)

It follows that in Gower, as distinct from earlier poets, Cupid is invariably blind: cf. his Latin poem *Ecce patet tensus ceci Cupidinis arcus* (*Works*, ed. G. C. Macaulay, iv. 358).

[2] Cf. his condemnation of the husband of the fair and virtuous wife, who yearns after other women: 'Men sein it is nou ofte so' (vi. 673). See further, 'Gower's Honeste Love', in *Patterns of Love and Courtesy* (1966).

It is thus that he meets the royal barge—probably near the very spot where an artist was later to show another love-poet, Charles d'Orléans, gazing from his prison in the White Tower. If he was no seafarer he evidently had the English liking for messing about in boats. He has the right nautical phrases for the 'topseilcole' or a following wind (v. 3119) or the distinctive craft of the Mediterranean (ii. 2543). Even his proverbial and figurative language smacks of the sea:

> The schip of love hath lost his rother
> So that he can no reson stere. . . . (ii. 2494–5)
>
> Whanne he berth lowest the seile
> Thanne is he swiftest to beguile. (i. 704–5)[1]

Gower's style is rarely more figurative than this; his other images depend chiefly on homely proverbial allusion—the book is rich in gnomic utterance. Though his protestation that 'I no rethorique have used' (viii. 3064*) is not to be taken wholly at its face value, it is true that in the English poem we do not have to 'climben over a heighe style'. Florid rhetorical effects are reserved for the elegaics of the *Vox Clamantis*.[2]

The shrill comminatory tone of that poem grows tedious long before we come to the end of its 22,000 lines; the occasional resort to the theme of *Dies Irae* in the later *Confessio* (e.g. ii. 3406 ff.) is far more effective. But the commination should not deafen us to the sustained metrical fluency of the Latin work. Longer poems in medieval Latin exist, but they are of earlier date and came out of the cloister, whereas Gower was a layman, probably not even a university man. His performance in this kind speaks highly for fourteenth-century schooling; and it prepared him to plan his English poem (which has its own admixture of various and epigrammatic Latin headpieces) on the same generous lines. His equally long, and equally unread, French poem, *Le Mirour de l'omme*, shows an expertise in rhymed verse that was to prove equally useful when he turned to 'boke som newe thing' in accordance with King Richard's behest (*CA* prol. 48* ff.).

---

[1] Cf. i. 1064–70, 1165; ii. 1880 ff., 2152, 2380; v. 3299, 3313; vi. 1422 (see Macaulay's note); viii. 1890 (n.) etc.; and note the realistic 'fish' image of the greedy luce, v. 2015 (n.). [2] But see iii. 276–86 (p. 25 below).

For this last and happiest work he chose the octosyllabic metre that his friend Chaucer had made a flexible instrument for narrative in the *Book of the Duchess* and the *House of Fame*. In the former of these poems Chaucer himself had put into rhyme Ovid's fable of Ceyx and Alcione as illustrative of 'the lawe of kinde' (*BD*, 52–56), and the latter shows him likewise in search of

> Somme newe thinges, y not what,
> Tydinges, other this or that,
> Of love, or such thinges glade. (*House of Fame*, 1887–9)

It is a curious coincidence that Chaucer's search led him to just such a throng of wayfarers as he was later to meet 'in Southwark at the Tabard as I lay'; in the very parish, to wit, where Gower lived, died, and was buried in the high Gothic tomb on which the allegorical figures of his cherished virtues Pity, Mercy, and Justice are still depicted in prayer for the repose of his soul.

If Gower is little read today it is as much because of the disappearance of the Gothic piety that those figures represent as because of his artistic limitations. The practice of the confessional, on which he erected his discrete architectonic, is no longer part of everyday experience, so that critics are prone to sense something indecorous in his adaptation of it to the office and affairs of love. In fact nothing (unless we may add to the canon the pleasing anonymous love-vision called *Le songe vert*)[1] shows his delicacy more clearly than the way he has transposed the language of priestly shrift into another key without anachronism or aesthetic or moral incongruity. Compared with the long cyclopaedic excursuses of *Le Roman de la Rose*, the discourse in Book v on the heathen gods or the *speculum* of knowledge in Book vii (ingeniously introduced to take Amans' mind off his troubles) hardly count as a digression; they should rather remind us that instruction was always part of his purpose: 'somdel for good aprise . . . I have it mad' (viii. 3060–2*). As for his rich variety of stories (as many come from medieval as from classical sources), handbooks for priests and penitents had for a century been recommending the use and study of *exempla* that would bring

---

[1] The poem is printed in *Romania* xxxiii. Miss E. Seaton argues for Gower's authorship in *Medium Aevum*, xix (1950), 1–16.

home the evils of the capital sins. To fit religious practice to the general relish for tales and love-doctrine was a brilliant stroke. And it is not being frivolous to say that in more than one sense Genius had a part in it.[1]

That the medieval appetite for stories was almost insatiable is suggested by an account in the *Flamenca* of forty-five tales told at a single wedding feast.[2] But it is highly unlikely that Gower expected his poem to be read continuously or that he would have been displeased by the anthologizing of his tales that began in the fifteenth century. The present selection does not claim to contain the best of his verse, but it does attempt to represent him at his best. Another volume could be filled with tales equally varied and equally worth the attention of the modern reader—e.g. 'The King of Hungary' (*CA*, i. 2021–253), 'Pygmalion' (iv. 371–436), 'Demophon and Phillis' (iv. 731–886), 'The King of Apulia' (v. 2643–826), 'Ulysses' (vi. 1391–767), 'Nectanabus' (vi. 1789–2336); and the tale of Constance (ii. 587–1600) stands up well, in general, when compared with Chaucer's Man of Law's more famous version of the story. Again, the long Prologue to the *Confessio* is not the less deserving of study because it is not easily excerptible. It should be read in Macaulay's edition of the complete *Works*—from which all the present selections are taken.

[1] The role of the priest Genius in the poem has been generally misunderstood. If there is something in him of Jean de Meun's *Genius*, there is more of Jean's *Nature*, and if there is a hint of Alain of Lille's priest there is also a hint of Spenser's deity in the Garden of Adonis, who 'ofte of secret ills bids us beware; That is our Selfe. . . .' For, as Lewis noted, by the end of the *Confessio* he has become '"the lover's deepest heart", telling him bitter truths, now no longer avoidable' (*The Allegory of Love*, p. 220). Like Amans his penitent, he is many-faceted; indeed he obliquely reflects the struggle between passion and reason, measure and excess, private interest and public weal, that takes place in all lovers and in all men. At the same time his humour bespeaks a shrewd and experienced confessor.

[2] The catalogue is printed by W. P. Ker in *Epic and Romance*, Note D (p. 384). It doubtless represents a poetic heightening of actual conditions.

BIOGRAPHICAL AND TEXTUAL NOTE

ABOUT Gower's life little can be said with certainty. The name is not uncommon in fourteenth-century records, and 'John Gower' is not necessarily the poet. His family evidently had Yorkshire origins, but some features of his language suggest a connexion with Kent, where he purchased lands in 1378. In that year Chaucer, when setting out for Italy, gave power of attorney to Gower and a lawyer called Richard Forester. In the *Mirour de l'omme* he says 'je ne suy pas clers . . . Ainz ai vestu la raye mancé' (21772-4): a reference to the distinctive dress of serjeants at law and certain court officials; and other documents and allusions confirm the suggestion that he was a Londoner versed in the law who was in touch with Kentish gentry, chose his friends chiefly from the legal and ecclesiastical professions, and had some knowledge of life at court. His ownership of Kentwell manor (Long Melford) indicates a connexion with Suffolk also.

His first major work was the *Mirour de l'omme*, or *Speculum Meditantis*, a didactic poem of which 29,444 lines survive, in twelve-line stanzas of French octosyllabics. In it he confesses that

> Jai trestout m'abandonoie
> Au foldelit et veine joye,
> Dont ma vesture desguisay
> Et les fols ditz d'amours fesoie
> Dont en chantant je carolloie (27337-41)

—in other words, that 'in the floures of his youthe' he had written love-ditties—like Chaucer (see p. 118 below), and like his own Amans, whom he was to represent as composing 'rondeal, balade, and virelai' (*CA*, i. 2709). Some of the fifty-one French balades that survive in the Trentham MS.[1] may represent these early poems. Machaut, Deschamps, and Froissart had made the balade a fashionable medium for love-poetry well before the death of Edward III (1377).

[1] Now B.M. Egerton MS. 2862.

Vox Clamantis, in 10,265 Latin elegaics, is essentially a mordant description of society in the following reign,[1] and includes (in its present form) accounts of the Peasants' Revolt (1381) and of Richard II's reconciliation with the London Commune (1392). The original (undated) Prologue and Conclusion to the third major poem, the *Confessio Amantis*, include a dedication to Richard, but in 1393 or thereabouts this was changed in favour of Henry of Lancaster, who in that year gave 'an esquire John Gower' the collar that is presumably the collar of SS shown on his tomb. Five weeks after his coronation, Henry rewarded Gower, who gives an account of his usurpation in the *Cronica Tripertita*—a Latin poem in 1,062 leonine hexameters, including thinly veiled heraldic references to the nobles who had opposed Richard—with a grant of two pipes of Gascon wine for life. The untitled English poem called by G. C. Macaulay 'In Praise of Peace' belongs to the same period (*c.* 1399–1400).

By 1398, and perhaps for some time earlier, Gower was living in the Priory of St. Mary Overy, Southwark. In that year the Bishop of Winchester granted a licence for his marriage to a fellow-parishioner Agnes Groundolf, whom the poet described in an epitaph as *uxor amans humilis*. She outlived him. Eighteen balades that often follow the *Confessio* in the manuscripts and that are devoted specifically to 'les amantz marietz' conclude with a couplet that links them with this marriage:

> Hinc vetus annorum Gower sub spe meritorum
> Ordine sponsorum tutus adhibo thorum.

These balades were given a Northern English form by an unknown scribe, *c.* 1402.[2]

In sending a copy of *Vox Clamantis* to Bishop Arundel about 1400 Gower described himself as *senex et cecus*; a man might be *senex* at forty (to Petrarch fifty-three was an advanced age), but other personal references in this *Epistola*, along with those at the end of the *Confessio* (see p. 115) indicate that he was probably over sixty by the turn of the century. His will was proved on 24 Oct. 1408. He left bequests, including a large *martilogium*,

---

[1] The title is taken from John i. 23.
[2] Ed. H. N. MacCracken, *Yorkshire Archeological Journal*, xx (1909), 33–51.

or calendar composed at his expense, to Southwark Priory, and established there a chantry in which his tomb (not now *in situ*) was set up.

The authoritative edition of his works by G. C. Macaulay (four vols., Oxford, 1899–1902) includes in vol. iv a full account of all the documentary evidence for Gower's biography then known. It is now supplemented by the second chapter ('Life Records') of John H. Fisher, *John Gower: Moral Philosopher and Friend of Chaucer* (New York, 1964; London, 1965). Macaulay provides an extended summary of the major works, and Eric W. Stockton describes and analyses the non-English poems in the Introduction to his translation of *The Major Latin Works* (Seattle, 1962). Macaulay's account of the manuscripts of the *Confessio* (as of those of the other poems) remains indispensable. Fisher discusses their relationships afresh (Chapter 3) and gives their present location in an Appendix.[1] Fisher also traces Gower's critical reputation, considers his 'major themes', and propounds a novel theory of the poet's influence on Chaucer. Like the other recent critics whose views Fisher cites and develops, he is chiefly concerned with the social and political significance of the French and Latin works; these are also the basis of the account of Gower's political theory in Arthur B. Ferguson, *The articulate Citizen and the English Renaissance*, Chapters 2 and 3 (Durham, N.C., 1965). Maria Wickert's *Studien zu John Gower* (Cologne, 1953) is devoted to *Vox Clamantis*—except for the sixth chapter, which considers the narrative technique of the *Confessio* as exemplified in the Tales of Actaeon, Pygmalion, and Florent.[2]

Macaulay's chapter on Gower in the Cambridge History of English Literature, vol. ii, remains a useful introduction to the English poems. The other chief studies of these are by W. P. Ker in *Essays on Medieval Literature* (London, 1901) and C. S. Lewis in *The Allegory of Love* (Oxford, 1936), Chapter V. To the miscellaneous items listed under *Gower* in the Cambridge Bibliography of English Literature and its Supplement may be added: P. Fison,

[1] But the Clumber MS. is now MS. Lyell 13 in the Bodleian Library.

[2] As Dr. Wickert's book is not easily accessible, a reference to the account of it in *The Review of English Studies*, N.S. viii (1957), 54, may be in order.

'The Poet in John Gower' (*Essays in Criticism*, viii (1958), 16–25;
Gavin Bone, 'Extant MSS. Printed by Wynkyn de Worde', *The
Library*, fourth series, xii (1931), 284–306: this article attempts
to show that the manuscript which is now Magd. Coll. Oxf. 213
was probably marked up by Caxton to guide the compositors of
his edition of the *Confessio* (1483);[1] John J. McNally, 'The
Penitential and Courtly Tradition in Gower's *Confessio Amantis*',
in *Studies in Medieval Culture*, edited by John R. Sommerfeldt,
Western University, Michigan (1964), pp. 74–94; Derek
Pearsall, 'Gower's narrative art', *PMLA*, lxxxi (1966), 475–84;
J. A. W. Bennett, 'Gower's *Honeste Love*', and J. Lawlor, 'On
Romanticism in the *Confessio Amantis*', in *Patterns of Love and
Courtesy*, edited by J. Lawlor, 1966; Donald Schueler, 'The Age of
the Lover in Gower's *Confessio Amantis*', *Medium Ævum*, xxxvi
(1967). The Balades are discussed by M. D. Legge, *Anglo-
Norman Literature and its background* (1963), pp. 357–61.

The Frontispieces, which are reproduced by permission of the
Curators of the Bodleian Library, are from Bodleian MSS. 294,
fol. 9 and 902, fol. 8. For the artists see Gereth M. Spriggs,
'Unnoticed Bodleian MSS. illuminated by Herman Scheerre and
his school', *Bodleian Library Record*, vii (1964), 193–203. The
spirit of the miniatures is strikingly different from the ironic
representations of similar scenes in manuscripts of the *Roman
de la Rose* (e.g. those repr. in figs. 94 and 96 of Rosemond
Tuve's *Allegorical Imagery* (1966)).

The Editor owes thanks to Mrs. Margaret Twycross for help
in preparing part of the Glossary.
Abbreviations in general follow the forms used in F. N.
Robinson's edition of Chaucer.

[1] But see now N. F. Blake in *Anglia*, 85 (1967), 282–93.

SELECTIONS FROM
CONFESSIO AMANTIS

I

Love and the Lover

Naturatus amor nature legibus orbem
Subdit, et vnanimes concitat esse feras:
Huius enim mundi Princeps amor esse videtur,
Cuius eget diues, pauper et omnis ope.
Sunt in agone pares amor et fortuna, que cecas
Plebis ad insidias vertit vterque rotas.
Est amor egra salus, vexata quies, pius error,
Bellica pax, vulnus dulce, suaue malum.

I MAY noght strecche up to the hevene
Min hand, ne setten al in evene
This world, which evere is in balance:
It stant noght in my sufficance
So grete thinges to compasse,
Bot I mot lete it overpasse
And treten upon othre thinges.
Forthi the stile of my writinges
Fro this day forth I thenke change
And speke of thing is noght so strange,   10
Which every kinde hath upon honde,
And wherupon the world mot stonde,
And hath don sithen it began,
And schal whil ther is any man;
And that is love, of which I mene
To trete, as after schal be sene.
In which ther can noman him reule,
For loves lawe is out of reule,
That of tomoche or of tolite

Welnyh is every man to wyte,   20
And natheles ther is noman
In al this world so wys, that can
Of love tempre the mesure,
Bot as it falth in aventure:
For wit ne strengthe may noght helpe,
And he which elles wolde him yelpe
Is rathest throwen under fote,
Ther can no wiht therof do bote.
For yet was nevere such covine,
That couthe ordeine a medicine   30
To thing which god in lawe of kinde
Hath set, for ther may noman finde
The rihte salve of such a sor.
It hath and schal ben everemor
That love is maister wher he wile,
Ther can no lif make other skile;
For wher as evere him lest to sette,
Ther is no myht which him may lette.
Bot what schal fallen ate laste,
The sothe can no wisdom caste,   40
Bot as it falleth upon chance;
For if ther evere was balance
Which of fortune stant governed,
I may wel lieve as I am lerned
That love hath that balance on honde,
Which wol no reson understonde.
For love is blind and may noght se,
Forthi may no certeinete
Be set upon his jugement,
Bot as the whiel aboute went   50
He yifth his graces undeserved,
And fro that man which hath him served
Fulofte he takth aweye his fees,
As he that pleieth ate dees,
And therupon what schal befalle
He not, til that the chance falle,
Wher he schal lese or he schal winne.

And thus fulofte men beginne,
That if thei wisten what it mente,
Thei wolde change al here entente. 60
   And forto proven it is so,
I am miselven on of tho,
Which to this scole am underfonge.
For it is siththe go noght longe,
As forto speke of this matiere,
I may you telle, if ye woll hiere,
A wonder hap which me befell,
That was to me bothe hard and fell,
Touchende of love and his fortune,
The which me liketh to comune 70
And pleinly forto telle it oute.
To hem that ben lovers aboute
Fro point to point I wol declare
And wryten of my woful care,
Mi wofull day, my wofull chance,
That men mowe take remembrance
Of that thei schall hierafter rede:
For in good feith this wolde I rede,
That every man ensample take
Of wisdom which him is betake, 80
And that he wot of good aprise
To teche it forth, for such emprise
Is forto preise; and therfore I
Woll wryte and schewe al openly
How love and I togedre mette,
Wherof the world ensample fette
Mai after this, whan I am go,
Of thilke unsely jolif wo,
Whos reule stant out of the weie,
Nou glad and nou gladnesse aweie, 90
And yet it may noght be withstonde
For oght that men may understonde.

Non ego Sampsonis vires, non Herculis arma
   Vinco, sum sed vt hii victus amore pari.

3

Vt discant alii, docet experiencia facti,
* Rebus in ambiguis que sit habenda via.*
Deuius ordo ducis temptata pericla sequentem
* Instruit a tergo, ne simul ille cadat.*
Me quibus ergo Venus, casus, laqueauit amantem,
* Orbis in exemplum scribere tendo palam.*

Upon the point that is befalle
Of love, in which that I am falle,
I thenke telle my matiere:
Now herkne, who that wol it hiere
Of my fortune how that it ferde.
This enderday, as I forthferde
To walke, as I yow telle may,—
And that was in the monthe of Maii,   100
Whan every brid hath chose his make
And thenkth his merthes forto make
Of love that he hath achieved;
Bot so was I nothing relieved,
For I was further fro my love
Than erthe is fro the hevene above,
As forto speke of eny sped:
So wiste I me non other red,
Bot as it were a man forfare
Unto the wode I gan to fare,   110
Noght forto singe with the briddes,
For whanne I was the wode amiddes,
I fond a swote grene pleine,
And ther I gan my wo compleigne
Wisshinge and wepinge al myn one,
For other merthes made I none.
So hard me was that ilke throwe,
That ofte sithes overthrowe
To grounde I was withoute breth;
And evere I wisshide after deth,   120
Whanne I out of my peine awok,
And caste up many a pitous lok
Unto the hevene, and seide thus:

4

'O thou Cupide, O thou Venus,
Thou god of love and thou goddesse,
Wher is pite? wher is meknesse?
Now doth me pleinly live or dye,
For certes such a maladie
As I now have and longe have hadd,
It myhte make a wisman madd,   130
If that it scholde longe endure.
O Venus, queene of loves cure,
Thou lif, thou lust, thou mannes hele,
Behold my cause and my querele,
And yif me som part of thi grace,
So that I may finde in this place
If thou be gracious or non.'

And with that word I sawh anon
The kyng of love and qweene bothe;
Bot he that kyng with yhen wrothe   140
His chiere aweiward fro me caste,
And forth he passede ate laste.
Bot natheles er he forth wente
A firy dart me thoghte he hente
And threw it thurgh myn herte rote:
In him fond I non other bote,
For lenger list him noght to duelle.
Bot sche that is the source and welle
Of wel or wo, that schal betide
To hem that loven, at that tide   150
Abod, bot forto tellen hiere
Sche cast on me no goodly chiere.
Thus natheles to me sche seide,
'What art thou, sone?' and I abreide
Riht as a man doth out of slep,
And therof tok sche riht good kep
And bad me nothing ben adrad:
Bot for al that I was noght glad,
For I ne sawh no cause why.
And eft scheo asketh, what was I: 160

5

I seide, 'A caitif that lith hiere:
What wolde ye, my ladi diere?
Schal I ben hol or elles dye?'
Sche seide, 'Tell thi maladie:
What is thi sor of which thou pleignest?
Ne hyd it noght, for if thou feignest,
I can do the no medicine.'
'Ma dame, I am a man of thyne,
That in thi court have longe served,
And aske that I have deserved,   170
Som wele after my longe wo.'
And sche began to loure tho,
And seide, 'Ther is manye of yow
Faitours, and so may be that thow
Art riht such on, and be feintise
Seist that thou hast me do servise.'
And natheles sche wiste wel,
Mi world stod on an other whiel
Withouten eny faiterie:
Bot algate of my maladie   180
Sche bad me telle and seie hir trowthe.
'My dame, if ye wolde have rowthe,'
Quod I, 'than wolde I telle yow.'
'Sey forth,' quod sche, 'and tell me how;
Schew me thi seknesse everydiel.'
'Ma dame, that can I do wel,
Be so my lif therto wol laste.'
With that hir lok on me sche caste,
And seide: 'In aunter if thou live,
Mi will is ferst that thou be schrive;   190
And natheles how that it is
I wot miself, bot for al this
Unto my prest, which comth anon,
I woll thou telle it on and on,
Bothe all thi thoght and al thi werk.
O Genius myn oghne clerk,
Com forth and hier this mannes schrifte,'
Quod Venus tho; and I uplifte

Min hefd with that, and gan beholde
The selve prest, which as sche wolde   200
Was redy there and sette him doun
To hiere my confessioun.

This worthi prest, this holy man
To me spekende thus began,
And seide: 'Benedicite,
Mi sone, of the felicite
Of love and ek of all the wo
Thou schalt thee schrive, of bothe tuo.
What thou er this for loves sake
Hast felt, let nothing be forsake,   210
Tell pleinliche as it is befalle.'
And with that word I gan doun falle
On knees, and with devocioun
And with full gret contricioun
I seide thanne: 'Dominus,
Min holi fader Genius,
So as thou hast experience
Of love, for whos reverence
Thou schalt me schriven at this time,
I prai the let me noght mistime   220
Mi schrifte, for I am destourbed
In al myn herte, and so contourbed,
That I ne may my wittes gete,
So schal I moche thing foryete:
Bot if thou wolt my schrifte oppose
Fro point to point, thanne I suppose,
Ther schal nothing be left behinde.
Bot now my wittes ben so blinde,
That I ne can miselven teche.'
Tho he began anon to preche,   230
And with his wordes debonaire
He seide tome softe and faire:
'Thi schrifte to oppose and hiere,
My sone, I am assigned hiere
Be Venus the godesse above,

7

Whos prest I am touchende of love.
Bot natheles for certein skile
I mot algate and nedes wile
Noght only make my spekynges
Of love, bot of othre thinges,   240
That touchen to the cause of vice.
For that belongeth to th'office
Of prest, whos ordre that I bere,
So that I wol nothing forbere,
That I the vices on and on
Ne schal thee schewen everychon;
Wherof thou myht take evidence
To reule with thi conscience.
Bot of conclusion final
Conclude I wol in special   250
For love, whos servant I am,
And why the cause is that I cam.
So thenke I to don bothe tuo,
Ferst that myn ordre longeth to,
The vices forto telle arewe,
Bot next above alle othre schewe
Of love I wol the propretes,
How that thei stonde be degrees
After the disposicioun
Of Venus, whos condicioun   260
I moste folwe, as I am holde.
For I with love am al withholde,
So that the lasse I am to wyte,
Thogh I ne conne bot a lyte
Of othre thinges that ben wise:
I am noght tawht in such a wise;
For it is noght my comun us
To speke of vices and vertus,
Bot al of love and of his lore,
For Venus bokes of nomore   270
Me techen nowther text ne glose.
Bot for als moche as I suppose
It sit a prest to be wel thewed,

And schame it is if he be lewed,
Of my presthode after the forme
I wol thi schrifte so enforme,
That ate leste thou schalt hiere
The vices, and to thi matiere
Of love I schal hem so remene,
That thou schalt knowe what thei mene.   280
For what a man schal axe or sein
Touchende of schrifte, it mot be plein,
It nedeth noght to make it queinte,
For trowthe hise wordes wol noght peinte:
That I wole axe of the forthi,
My Sone, it schal be so pleinly,
That thou schalt knowe and understonde
The pointz of schrifte how that thei stonde.'

II

The Tale of Florent (i. 1406–1861)

Confessor   THER was whilom be daies olde
A worthi knyht, and as men tolde
He was nevoeu to th'emperour
And of his court a courteour: 1410
Wifles he was, Florent he hihte,
He was a man that mochel myhte;
Of armes he was desirous,
Chivalerous and amorous,
And for the fame of worldes speche,
Strange aventures forto seche,
He rod the marches al aboute.
And fell a time, as he was oute,
Fortune, which may every thred
Tobreke and knette of mannes sped,   1420
Schop, as this knyht rod in a pas,
That he be strengthe take was,
And to a castell thei him ladde,
Wher that he fewe frendes hadde:

For so it fell that ilke stounde
That he hath with a dedly wounde
Feihtende his oghne hondes slain
Branchus, which to the Capitain
Was sone and heir, wherof ben wrothe
The fader and the moder bothe.   1430
That knyht Branchus was of his hond
The worthieste of al his lond,
And fain thei wolden do vengance
Upon Florent, bot remembrance
That thei toke of his worthinesse
Of knyhthod and of gentilesse,
And how he stod of cousinage
To th'emperour, made hem assuage,
And dorsten noght slen him for fere:
In gret desputeisoun thei were   1440
Among hemself, what was the beste.
Ther was a lady, the slyheste
Of alle that men knewe tho,
So old sche myhte unethes go,
And was grantdame unto the dede:
And sche with that began to rede,   ·
And seide how sche wol bringe him inne,
That sche schal him to dethe winne
Al only of his oghne grant,
Thurgh strengthe of verray covenant   1450
Withoute blame of eny wiht.
Anon sche sende for this kniht,
And of hire sone sche alleide
The deth, and thus to him sche seide:
'Florent, how so thou be to wyte
Of Branchus deth, men schal respite
As now to take vengement,
Be so thou stonde in juggement
Upon certein condicioun,
That thou unto a questioun   1460
Which I schal axe schalt ansuere;
And over this thou schalt ek swere,

That if thou of the sothe faile,
Ther schal non other thing availe,
That thou ne schalt thi deth receive.
And for men schal thee noght deceive,
That thou therof myht ben avised,
Thou schalt have day and tyme assised
And leve saufly forto wende,
Be so that at thi daies ende   1470
Thou come ayein with thin avys.'
   This knyht, which worthi was and wys,
This lady preith that he may wite,
And have it under seales write,
What questioun it scholde be
For which he schal in that degree
Stonde of his lif in jeupartie.
With that sche feigneth compaignie,
And seith: 'Florent, on love it hongeth
Al that to myn axinge longeth: 1480
What alle wommen most desire,
This wole I axe, and in th'empire
Wher as thou hast most knowlechinge
Tak conseil upon this axinge.'
   Florent this thing hath undertake,
The day was set, the time take,
Under his seal he wrot his oth,
In such a wise and forth he goth
Hom to his emes court ayein;
To whom his aventure plein   1490
He tolde, of that him is befalle.
And upon that thei weren alle
The wiseste of the lond asent,
Bot natheles of on assent
Thei myhte noght acorde plat,
On seide this, an othre that.
After the disposicioun
Of naturel complexioun
To som womman it is plesance,
That to an other is grevance;   1500

Bot such a thing in special,
Which to hem alle in general
Is most plesant, and most desired
Above alle othre and most conspired,
Such o thing conne thei noght finde
Be constellacion ne kinde:
And thus Florent withoute cure
Mot stonde upon his aventure,
And is al schape unto the lere,
As in defalte of his answere.   1510

   This knyht hath levere forto dye
Than breke his trowthe and forto lye
In place ther as he was swore,
And schapth him gon ayein therfore.
Whan time cam he tok his leve,
That lengere wolde he noght beleve,
And preith his em he be noght wroth,
For that is a point of his oth,
He seith, that noman schal him wreke,
Thogh afterward men hiere speke   1520
That he par aventure deie.
And thus he wente forth his weie
Alone as knyht aventurous,
And in his thoght was curious
To wite what was best to do:
And as he rod al one so,
And cam nyh ther he wolde be,
In a forest under a tre
He syh wher sat a creature,
A lothly wommannysch figure,   1530
That forto speke of fleisch and bon
So foul yit syh he nevere non.
This knyht behield hir redely,
And as he wolde have passed by,
Sche cleped him and bad abide;
And he his horse heved aside
Tho torneth, and to hire he rod,
And there he hoveth and abod,

To wite what sche wolde mene.
And sche began him to bemene,   1540
And seide: 'Florent be thi name,
Thou hast on honde such a game,
That bot thou be the betre avised,
Thi deth is schapen and devised,
That al the world ne mai the save,
Bot if that thou my conseil have.'
  Florent, whan he this tale herde,
Unto this olde wyht answerde
And of hir conseil he hir preide.
And sche ayein to him thus seide: 1550
'Florent, if I for the so schape,
That thou thurgh me thi deth ascape
And take worschipe of thi dede,
What schal I have to my mede?'
'What thing,' quod he, 'that thou wolt axe.'
'I bidde nevere a betre taxe,'
Quod sche, 'bot ferst, er thou be sped,
Thou schalt me leve such a wedd,
That I wol have thi trowthe in honde
That thou schalt be myn housebonde.'   1560
'Nay,' seith Florent, 'that may noght be.'
'Ryd thanne forth thi wey,' quod sche,
'And if thou go withoute red,
Thou schalt be sekerliche ded.'
Florent behihte hire good ynowh
Of lond, of rente, of park, of plowh,
Bot al that compteth sche at noght.
Tho fell this knyht in mochel thoght,
Now goth he forth, now comth ayein,
He wot noght what is best to sein,   1570
And thoghte, as he rod to and fro,
That chese he mot on of the tuo,
Or forto take hire to his wif
Or elles forto lese his lif.
And thanne he caste his avantage,
That sche was of so gret an age,

That sche mai live bot a while,
And thoghte put hire in an ile,
Wher that noman hire scholde knowe,
Til sche with deth were overthrowe.   1580
And thus this yonge lusti knyht
Unto this olde lothly wiht
Tho seide: 'If that non other chance
Mai make my deliverance,
Bot only thilke same speche
Which, as thou seist, thou schalt me teche,
Have hier myn hond, I schal thee wedde.'
And thus his trowthe he leith to wedde.
With that sche frounceth up the browe:
'This covenant I wol allowe,'   1590
Sche seith: 'if eny other thing
Bot that thou hast of my techyng
Fro deth thi body mai respite,
I woll thee of thi trowthe acquite,
And elles be non other weie.
Now herkne me what I schal seie.
Whan thou art come into the place,
Wher now thei maken gret manace
And upon thi comynge abyde,
Thei wole anon the same tide   1600
Oppose thee of thin answere.
I wot thou wolt nothing forbere
Of that thou wenest be thi beste,
And if thou myht so finde reste,
Wel is, for thanne is ther nomore.
And elles this schal be my lore,
That thou schalt seie, upon this molde
That alle wommen lievest wolde
Be soverein of mannes love:
For what womman is so above,   1610
Sche hath, as who seith, al hire wille;
And elles may sche noght fulfille
What thing hir were lievest have.
With this answere thou schalt save

14

Thiself, and other wise noght.
And whan thou hast thin ende wroght,
Com hier ayein, thou schalt me finde,
And let nothing out of thi minde.'
He goth him forth with hevy chiere,
As he that not in what manere   1620
He mai this worldes joie atteigne:
For if he deie, he hath a peine,
And if he live, he mot him binde
To such on which of alle kinde
Of wommen is th'unsemlieste:
Thus wot he noght what is the beste:
Bot be him lief or be him loth,
Unto the castell forth he goth
His full answere forto yive,
Or forto deie or forto live.   1630
Forth with his conseil cam the lord,
The thinges stoden of record,
He sende up for the lady sone,
And forth sche cam, that olde mone.
In presence of the remenant
The strengthe of al the covenant
Tho was reherced openly,
And to Florent sche bad forthi
That he schal tellen his avis,
As he that woot what is the pris.   1640
Florent seith al that evere he couthe,
Bot such word cam ther non to mowthe,
That he for yifte or for beheste
Mihte eny wise his deth areste.
And thus he tarieth longe and late,
Til that this lady bad algate
That he schal for the dom final
Yive his answere in special
Of that sche hadde him ferst opposed:
And thanne he hath trewly supposed   1650
That he him may of nothing yelpe,
Bot if so be tho wordes helpe,

15

Whiche as the womman hath him tawht;
Wherof he hath an hope cawht
That he schal ben excused so,
And tolde out plein his wille tho.
And whan that this matrone herde
The manere how this knyht ansuerde,
Sche seide: 'Ha treson, wo thee be,
That hast thus told the privite,   1660
Which alle wommen most desire!
I wolde that thou were afire.'
Bot natheles in such a plit
Florent of his answere is quit:
And tho began his sorwe newe,
For he mot gon, or ben untrewe,
To hire which his trowthe hadde.
Bot he, which alle schame dradde,
Goth forth in stede of his penance,
And takth the fortune of his chance,   1670
As he that was with trowthe affaited.
   This olde wyht him hath awaited
In place wher as he hire lefte:
Florent his wofull heved uplefte
And syh this vecke wher sche sat,
Which was the lothlieste what
That evere man caste on his yhe:
Hire nase bass, hire browes hyhe,
Hire yhen smale and depe set,
Hire chekes ben with teres wet,   1680
And rivelen as an emty skyn
Hangende doun unto the chin,
Hire lippes schrunken ben for age,
Ther was no grace in the visage,
Hir front was nargh, hir lockes hore,
Sche loketh forth as doth a More,
Hire necke is schort, hir schuldres courbe,
That myhte a mannes lust destourbe,
Hire body gret and nothing smal,
And schortly to descrive hire al,   1690

Sche hath no lith withoute a lak;
Bot lich unto the wollesak
Sche proferth hire unto this knyht,
And bad him, as he hath behyht,
So as sche hath ben his warant,
That he hire holde covenant,
And be the bridel sche him seseth.
Bot godd wot how that sche him pleseth
Of suche wordes as sche spekth:
Him thenkth welnyh his herte brekth   1700
For sorwe that he may noght fle,
Bot if he wolde untrewe be.

    Loke how a sek man for his hele
Takth baldemoine with canele,
And with the mirre takth the sucre,
Ryht upon such a maner lucre
Stant Florent, as in this diete:
He drinkth the bitre with the swete,
He medleth sorwe with likynge,
And liveth, as who seith, deyinge;   1710
His youthe schal be cast aweie
Upon such on which as the weie
Is old and lothly overal.
Bot nede he mot that nede schal:
He wolde algate his trowthe holde,
As every knyht therto is holde,
What happ so evere him is befalle:
Thogh sche be the fouleste of alle,
Yet to th'onour of wommanhiede
Him thoghte he scholde taken hiede;   1720
So that for pure gentilesse,
As he hire couthe best adresce,
In ragges as sche was totore,
He set hire on his hors tofore
And forth he takth his weie softe;
No wonder thogh he siketh ofte.
Bot as an oule fleth be nyhte
Out of alle othre briddes syhte,

Riht so this knyht on daies brode
In clos him hield, and schop his rode   1730
On nyhtes time, til the tyde
That he cam there he wolde abide;
And prively withoute noise
He bringth this foule grete coise
To his castell in such a wise
That noman myhte hire schappe avise,
Til sche into the chambre cam:
Wher he his prive conseil nam
Of suche men as he most troste,
And tolde hem that he nedes moste   1740
This beste wedde to his wif,
For elles hadde he lost his lif.
  The prive wommen were asent,
That scholden ben of his assent:
Hire ragges thei anon of drawe,
And, as it was that time lawe,
She hadde bath, sche hadde reste,
And was arraied to the beste.
Bot with no craft of combes brode
Thei myhte hire hore lockes schode,   1750
And sche ne wolde noght be schore
For no conseil, and thei therfore,
With such atyr as tho was used,
Ordeinen that it was excused,
And hid so crafteliche aboute,
That noman myhte sen hem oute.
Bot when sche was fulliche arraied
And hire atyr was al assaied,
Tho was sche foulere on to se:
Bot yit it may non other be,   1760
Thei were wedded in the nyht;
So wo begon was nevere knyht
As he was thanne of mariage.
And sche began to pleie and rage,
As who seith, I am wel ynowh;
Bot he therof nothing ne lowh,

For sche tok thanne chiere on honde
And clepeth him hire housebonde,
And seith, 'My lord, go we to bedde,
For I to that entente wedde,   1770
That thou schalt be my worldes blisse:'
And profreth him with that to kisse,
As sche a lusti lady were.
His body myhte wel be there,
Bot as of thoght and of memoire
His herte was in purgatoire.
Bot yit for strengthe of matrimoine
He myhte make non essoine,
That he ne mot algates plie
To gon to bedde of compaignie: 1780
And whan thei were abedde naked,
Withoute slep he was awaked;
He torneth on that other side,
For that he wolde hise yhen hyde
Fro lokynge on that foule wyht.
The chambre was al full of lyht,
The courtins were of cendal thinne,
This newe bryd which lay withinne,
Thogh it be noght with his acord,
In armes sche beclipte hire lord,   1790
And preide, as he was torned fro,
He wolde him torne ayeinward tho;
'For now,' sche seith, 'we ben bothe on.'
And he lay stille as eny ston,
Bot evere in on sche spak and preide,
And bad him thenke on that he seide,
Whan that he tok hire be the hond.
   He herde and understod the bond,
How he was set to his penance,
And as it were a man in trance   1800
He torneth him al sodeinly,
And syh a lady lay him by
Of eyhtetiene wynter age,
Which was the faireste of visage

That evere in al this world he syh:
And as he wolde have take hire nyh,
Sche put hire hand and be his leve
Besoghte him that he wolde leve,
And seith that forto wynne or lese
He mot on of tuo thinges chese,   1810
Wher he wol have hire such on nyht,
Or elles upon daies lyht,
For he schal noght have bothe tuo.
And he began to sorwe tho,
In many a wise and caste his thoght,
Bot for al that yit cowthe he noght
Devise himself which was the beste.
And sche, that wolde his hertes reste,
Preith that he scholde chese algate,
Til ate laste longe and late   1820
He seide: 'O ye, my lyves hele,
Sey what you list in my querele,
I not what ansuere I schal yive:
Bot evere whil that I may live,
I wol that ye be my maistresse,
For I can noght miselve gesse
Which is the beste unto my chois.
Thus grante I yow myn hole vois,
Ches for ous bothen, I you preie;
And what as evere that ye seie,   1830
Riht as ye wole so wol I.'
    'Mi lord,' sche seide, 'grant merci,
For of this word that ye now sein,
That ye have mad me soverein,
Mi destine is overpassed,
That nevere hierafter schal be lassed
Mi beaute, which that I now have,
Til I be take into my grave;
Bot nyht and day as I am now
I schal alwey be such to yow.   1840
The kinges dowhter of Cizile
I am, and fell bot siththe awhile,

20

As I was with my fader late,
That my stepmoder for an hate,
Which toward me sche hath begonne,
Forschop me, til I hadde wonne
The love and sovereinete
Of what knyht that in his degre
Alle othre passeth of good name:
And, as men sein, ye ben the same,   1850
The dede proeveth it is so;
Thus am I youres evermo.'
Tho was plesance and joye ynowh,
Echon with other pleide and lowh;
Thei live longe and wel thei ferde,
And clerkes that this chance herde
Thei writen it in evidence,
To teche how that obedience
Mai wel fortune a man to love
And sette him in his lust above,   1860
As it befell unto this knyht.

III

The Tale of Canace (iii. 143–356)

THER was a king which Eolus
Was hote, and it befell him thus,
That he tuo children hadde faire,
The sone cleped was Machaire,
The dowhter ek Canace hihte.
Be daie bothe and ek be nyhte,
Whil thei be yonge, of comun wone
In chambre thei togedre wone,   150
And as thei scholden pleide hem ofte,
Til thei be growen up alofte
Into the youthe of lusti age,
Whan kinde assaileth the corage
With love and doth him forto bowe,

That he no reson can allowe,
Bot halt the lawes of nature:
For whom that love hath under cure,
As he is blind himself, riht so
He makth his client blind also.   160
In such manere as I you telle
As thei al day togedre duelle,
This brother mihte it noght asterte
That he with al his hole herte
His love upon his soster caste:
And so it fell hem ate laste,
That this Machaire with Canace
Whan thei were in a prive place,
Cupide bad hem ferst to kesse,
And after sche which is Maistresse   170
In kinde and techeth every lif
Withoute lawe positif,
Of which sche takth nomaner charge,
Bot kepth hire lawes al at large,
Nature, tok hem into lore
And tawht hem so, that overmore
Sche hath hem in such wise daunted,
That thei were, as who seith, enchaunted.
And as the blinde an other ledeth
And til thei falle nothing dredeth,   180
Riht so thei hadde non insihte;
Bot as the bridd which wole alihte
And seth the mete and noght the net,
Which in deceipte of him is set,
This yonge folk no peril sihe,
Bot that was likinge in here yhe,
So that thei felle upon the chance
Where witt hath lore his remembrance.
So longe thei togedre assemble,
The wombe aros, and sche gan tremble,   190
And hield hire in hire chambre clos
For drede it scholde be disclos
And come to hire fader ere:

22

Wherof the sone hadde also fere,
And feigneth cause forto ryde;
For longe dorste he noght abyde,
In aunter if men wolde sein
That he his soster hath forlein:
For yit sche hadde it noght beknowe
Whos was the child at thilke throwe.   200
Machaire goth, Canace abit,
The which was noght delivered yit,
Bot riht sone after that sche was.

   Now lest and herkne a woful cas.
The sothe, which mai noght ben hid,
Was ate laste knowe and kid
Unto the king, how that it stod.
And whan that he it understod,
Anon into malencolie,
As thogh it were a frenesie,   210
He fell, as he which nothing cowthe
How maistrefull love is in yowthe:
And for he was to love strange,
He wolde noght his herte change
To be benigne and favorable
To love, bot unmerciable
Betwen the wawe of wod and wroth
Into his dowhtres chambre he goth,
And sih the child was late bore,
Wherof he hath hise othes swore   220
That sche it schal ful sore abye.
And sche began merci to crie,
Upon hire bare knes and preide,
And to hire fader thus sche seide:
'Ha mercy! fader, thenk I am
Thi child, and of thi blod I cam.
That I misdede, yowthe it made,
And in the flodes bad me wade,
Wher that I sih no peril tho:
Bot now it is befalle so,   230
Merci, my fader, do no wreche!'

And with that word sche loste speche
And fell doun swounende at his fot,
As sche for sorwe nedes mot.
Bot his horrible crualte
Ther mihte attempre no pite:
Out of hire chambre forth he wente
Al full of wraththe in his entente,
And tok the conseil in his herte
That sche schal noght the deth asterte,   240
As he which malencolien
Of pacience hath no lien,
Wherof his wraththe he mai restreigne.
And in this wilde wode peine,
Whanne al his resoun was untame,
A kniht he clepeth be his name,
And tok him as be weie of sonde
A naked swerd to bere on honde,
And seide him that he scholde go
And telle unto his dowhter so   250
In the manere as he him bad,
How sche that scharpe swerdes blad
Receive scholde and do withal
So as sche wot wherto it schal.
Forth in message goth this kniht
Unto this wofull yonge wiht,
This scharpe swerd to hire he tok:
Wherof that al hire bodi qwok,
For wel sche wiste what it mente,
And that it was to thilke entente   260
That sche hireselven scholde slee.
And to the kniht sche seide: 'Yee,
Now that I wot my fadres wille,
That I schal in this wise spille,
I wole obeie me therto,
And as he wole it schal be do.
Bot now this thing mai be non other,
I wole a lettre unto mi brother,
So as my fieble hand may wryte,

With al my wofull herte endite.'   270
Sche tok a penne on honde tho,
Fro point to point and al the wo,
Als ferforth as hireself it wot,
Unto hire dedly frend sche wrot,
And tolde how that hire fader grace
Sche mihte for nothing pourchace;
And overthat, as thou schalt hiere,
Sche wrot and seide in this manere:
'O thou my sorwe and my gladnesse,
O thou myn hele and my siknesse,   280
O my wanhope and al my trust,
O my desese and al my lust,
O thou my wele, o thou my wo,
O thou my frend, o thou my fo,
O thou my love, o thou myn hate,
For thee mot I be ded algate.
Thilke ende may I noght asterte,
And yit with al myn hole herte,
Whil that me lasteth eny breth,
I wol the love into my deth.   290
Bot of o thing I schal thee preie,
If that my litel sone deie,
Let him be beried in my grave
Beside me, so schalt thou have
Upon ous bothe remembrance.
For thus it stant of my grevance;
Now at this time, as thou schalt wite,
With teres and with enke write
This lettre I have in cares colde:
In my riht hond my penne I holde,   300
And in my left the swerd I kepe,
And in my barm ther lith to wepe
Thi child and myn, which sobbeth faste.
Now am I come unto my laste:
Fare wel, for I schal sone deie,
And thenk how I thi love abeie.'
The pomel of the swerd to grounde

Sche sette, and with the point a wounde
Thurghout hire herte anon sche made,
And forth with that al pale and fade   310
Sche fell doun ded fro ther sche stod.
The child lay bathende in hire blod,
Out rolled fro the moder barm,
And for the blod was hot and warm,
He basketh him aboute thrinne.
Ther was no bote forto winne,
For he, which can no pite knowe,
The king, cam in the same throwe,
And sih how that his dowhter dieth
And how this babe al blody crieth;   320
Bot al that mihte him noght suffise,
That he ne bad to do juise
Upon the child, and bere him oute,
And seche in the forest aboute
Som wilde place, what it were,
To caste him out of honde there,
So that som beste him mai devoure,
Where as noman him schal socoure.
Al that he bad was don in dede:
Ha, who herde evere singe or rede   330
Of such a thing as that was do?
Bot he which ladde his wraththe so
Hath knowe of love bot a lite;
Bot for al that he was to wyte,
Thurgh his sodein malencolie
To do so gret a felonie.

    Forthi, my Sone, how so it stonde,
Be this cas thou miht understonde
That if thou evere in cause of love
Schalt deme, and thou be so above   340
That thou miht lede it at thi wille,
Let nevere thurgh thi wraththe spille
Which every kinde scholde save.
For it sit every man to have
Reward to love and to his miht,

26

Ayein whos strengthe mai no wiht:
And siththe an herte is so constreigned,
The reddour oghte be restreigned
To him that mai no bet aweie,
Whan he mot to Nature obeie.   350
For it is seid thus overal,
That nedes mot that nede schal
Of that a lif doth after kinde,
Wherof he mai no bote finde.
What nature hath set in hir lawe
Ther mai no mannes miht withdrawe.

IV

Idleness in love; the Tale of Rosiphelee; love and arms
(iv. 1083–1501; 1615–1770)

AMONG these othre of Slowthes kinde,
Which alle labour set behinde,
And hateth alle besinesse,
Ther is yit on, which Ydelnesse
Is cleped, and is the norrice
In mannes kinde of every vice,
Which secheth eases manyfold.
In wynter doth he noght for cold,   1090
In somer mai he noght for hete;
So whether that he frese or swete,
Or he be inne, or he be oute,
He wol ben ydel al aboute,
Bot if he pleie oght ate dees.
For who as evere take fees
And thenkth worschipe to deserve,
Ther is no lord whom he wol serve,
As forto duelle in his servise,
Bot if it were in such a wise,   1100
Of that he seth per aventure

27

That be lordschipe and coverture
He mai the more stonde stille,
And use his ydelnesse at wille.
For he ne wol no travail take
To ryde for his ladi sake,
Bot liveth al upon his wisshes;
And as a cat wolde ete fisshes
Withoute wetinge of his cles,
So wolde he do, bot natheles   1110
He faileth ofte of that he wolde.
   Mi sone, if thou of such a molde
Art mad, now tell me plein thi schrifte.

Amans   Nay, fader, god I yive a yifte,
That toward love, as be mi wit,
Al ydel was I nevere yit,
Ne nevere schal, whil I mai go.

Confessor   Now, sone, tell me thanne so,
What hast thou don of besischipe
To love and to the ladischipe   1120
Of hire which thi ladi is?

Amans   Mi fader, evere yit er this
In every place, in every stede,
What so mi lady hath me bede,
With al myn herte obedient
I have therto be diligent.
And if so is sche bidde noght,
What thing that thanne into my thoght
Comth ferst of that I mai suffise,
I bowe and profre my servise,   1130
Somtime in chambre, somtime in halle,
Riht as I se the times falle.
And whan sche goth to hiere masse,
That time schal noght overpasse,
That I n'aproche hir ladihede,
In aunter if I mai hire lede
Unto the chapelle and ayein.
Thanne is noght al mi weie in vein,
Somdeil I mai the betre fare,

28

Whan I, that mai noght fiele hir bare,   1140
Mai lede hire clothed in myn arm:
Bot afterward it doth me harm
Of pure ymaginacioun;
For thanne this collacioun
I make unto miselven ofte,
And seie, 'Ha lord, hou sche is softe,
How sche is round, hou sche is smal!
Now wolde god I hadde hire al
Withoute danger at mi wille!'
And thanne I sike and sitte stille,   1150
Of that I se mi besi thoght
Is torned ydel into noght.
Bot for al that lete I ne mai,
Whanne I se time an other dai,
That I ne do my besinesse
Unto mi ladi worthinesse.
For I therto mi wit afaite
To se the times and awaite
What is to done and what to leve:
And so, whan time is, be hir leve,   1160
What thing sche bit me don, I do,
And wher sche bidt me gon, I go,
And whanne hir list to clepe, I come.
Thus hath sche fulliche overcome
Min ydelnesse til I sterve,
So that I mot hire nedes serve,
For as men sein, nede hath no lawe.
Thus mot I nedly to hire drawe,
I serve, I bowe, I loke, I loute,
Min yhe folweth hire aboute,   1170
What so sche wole so wol I,
Whan sche wol sitte, I knele by,
And whan sche stant, than wol I stonde:
Bot whan sche takth hir werk on honde
Of wevinge or enbrouderie,
Than can I noght bot muse and prie
Upon hir fingres longe and smale,

And now I thenke, and now I tale,
And now I singe, and now I sike,
And thus mi contienance I pike.   1180
And if it falle, as for a time
Hir liketh noght abide bime,
Bot besien hire on other thinges,
Than make I othre tariinges
To dreche forth the longe dai,
For me is loth departe away.
And thanne I am so simple of port,
That forto feigne som desport
I pleie with hire litel hound
Now on the bedd, now on the ground,   1190
Now with hir briddes in the cage;
For ther is non so litel page,
Ne yit so simple a chamberere,
That I ne make hem alle chere,
Al for thei scholde speke wel:
Thus mow ye sen mi besi whiel,
That goth noght ydeliche aboute.
And if hir list to riden oute
On pelrinage or other stede,
I come, thogh I be noght bede,   1200
And take hire in min arm alofte
And sette hire in hire sadel softe,
And so forth lede hire be the bridel,
For that I wolde noght ben ydel.
And if hire list to ride in char,
And thanne I mai therof be war,
Anon I schape me to ryde
Riht evene be the chares side;
And as I mai, I speke among,
And otherwhile I singe a song,   1210
Which Ovide in his bokes made,
And seide, 'O whiche sorwes glade,
O which wofull prosperite
Belongeth to the proprete
Of love, who so wole him serve!

And yit therfro mai noman swerve,
That he ne mot his lawe obeie.'
And thus I ryde forth mi weie,
And am riht besi overal
With herte and with mi body al,   1220
As I have said you hier tofore.
My goode fader, tell therfore,
Of Ydelnesse if I have gilt.

Confessor   Mi sone, bot thou telle wilt
Oght elles than I mai now hiere,
Thou schalt have no penance hiere.
And natheles a man mai se,
How now adayes that ther be
Ful manye of suche hertes slowe,
That wol noght besien hem to knowe   1230
What thing love is, til ate laste,
That he with strengthe hem overcaste,
That malgre hem thei mote obeie
And don al ydelschipe aweie,
To serve wel and besiliche.
Bot, sone, thou art non of swiche,
For love schal the wel excuse:
Bot otherwise, if thou refuse
To love, thou miht so per cas
Ben ydel, as somtime was   1240
A kinges dowhter unavised,
Til that Cupide hire hath chastised:
Wherof thou schalt a tale hiere
Acordant unto this matiere.

    Of Armenye, I rede thus,
Ther was a king, which Herupus
Was hote, and he a lusti maide
To dowhter hadde, and as men saide
Hire name was Rosiphelee;
Which tho was of gret renomee,   1250
For sche was bothe wys and fair
And scholde ben hire fader hair.
Bot sche hadde o defalte of Slowthe

31

Towardes love, and that was rowthe;
For so wel cowde noman seie,
Which mihte sette hire in the weie
Of loves occupacion
Thurgh non ymaginacion;
That scole wolde sche noght knowe.
And thus sche was on of the slowe   1260
As of such hertes besinesse,
Til whanne Venus the goddesse,
Which loves court hath forto reule,
Hath broght hire into betre reule,
Forth with Cupide and with his miht:
For thei merveille how such a wiht,
Which tho was in hir lusti age,
Desireth nother mariage
Ne yit the love of paramours,
Which evere hath be the comun cours   1270
Amonges hem that lusti were.
So was it schewed after there:
For he that hihe hertes loweth
With fyri dartes whiche he throweth,
Cupide, which of love is godd,
In chastisinge hath mad a rodd
To dryve awei hir wantounesse;
So that withinne a while, I gesse,
Sche hadde on such a chance sporned,
That al hire mod was overtorned,   1280
Which ferst sche hadde of slow manere:
For thus it fell, as thou schalt hiere.
Whan come was the monthe of Maii,
Sche wolde walke upon a dai,
And that was er the sonne ariste;
Of wommen bot a fewe it wiste,
And forth sche wente prively
Unto the park was faste by,
Al softe walkende on the gras,
Til sche cam ther the launde was,   1290
Thurgh which ther ran a gret rivere.

It thoghte hir fair, and seide, 'Here
I wole abide under the schawe':
And bad hire wommen to withdrawe,
And ther sche stod al one stille,
To thenke what was in hir wille.
Sche sih the swote floures springe,
Sche herde glade foules singe,
Sche sih the bestes in her kinde,
The buck, the do, the hert, the hinde,   1300
The madle go with the femele;
And so began ther a querele
Betwen love and hir oghne herte,
Fro which sche couthe noght asterte.
And as sche caste hire yhe aboute,
Sche syh clad in o suite a route
Of ladis, wher thei comen ryde
Along under the wodes syde:
On faire amblende hors thei sete,
That were al whyte, fatte and grete,   1310
And everichon thei ride on side.
The sadles were of such a pride,
With perle and gold so wel begon,
So riche syh sche nevere non;
In kertles and in copes riche
Thei weren clothed, alle liche,
Departed evene of whyt and blew;
With alle lustes that sche knew
Thei were enbrouded overal.
Here bodies weren long and smal,   1320
The beaute faye upon her face
Non erthly thing it may desface;
Corones on here hed thei beere,
As ech of hem a qweene weere,
That al the gold of Cresus halle
The leste coronal of alle
Ne mihte have boght after the worth:
Thus come thei ridende forth.
    The kinges dowhter, which this syh,

For pure abaissht drowh hire adryh   1330
And hield hire clos under the bowh,
And let hem passen stille ynowh;
For as hire thoghte in hire avis,
To hem that were of such a pris
Sche was noght worthi axen there,
Fro when they come or what thei were:
Bot levere than this worldes good
Sche wolde have wist hou that it stod,
And putte hire hed alitel oute;
And as sche lokede hire aboute,   1340
Sche syh comende under the linde
A womman up an hors behinde.
The hors on which sche rod was blak,
Al lene and galled on the back,
And haltede, as he were encluyed,
Wherof the womman was annuied;
Thus was the hors in sori plit,
Bot for al that a sterre whit
Amiddes in the front he hadde.
Hir sadel ek was wonder badde,   1350
In which the wofull womman sat,
And natheles ther was with that
A riche bridel for the nones
Of gold and preciouse stones.
Hire cote was somdiel totore;
Aboute hir middel twenty score
Of horse haltres and wel mo
Ther hyngen ate time tho.
    Thus whan sche cam the ladi nyh,
Than tok sche betre hiede, and syh   1360
This womman fair was of visage,
Freyssh, lusti, yong and of tendre age;
And so this ladi, ther sche stod,
Bethoghte hire wel and understod
That this, which com ridende tho,
Tidinges couthe telle of tho
Which as sche sih tofore ryde,

34

And putte hir forth and preide abide,
And seide, 'Ha, suster, let me hiere,
What ben thei, that now riden hiere,   1370
And ben so richeliche arraied?'
    This womman, which com so esmaied,
Ansuerde with ful softe speche,
And seith, 'Ma dame, I schal you teche.
These ar of tho that whilom were
Servantz to love, and trowthe beere,
Ther as thei hadde here herte set.
Fare wel, for I mai noght be let:
Ma dame, I go to mi servise,
So moste I haste in alle wise;   1380
Forthi, ma dame, yif me leve,
I mai noght longe with you leve.'
    'Ha, goode soster, yit I preie,
Tell me whi ye ben so beseie
And with these haltres thus begon.'
    'Ma dame, whilom I was on
That to mi fader hadde a king;
Bot I was slow, and for no thing
Me liste noght to love obeie,
And that I now ful sore abeie.   1390
For I whilom no love hadde,
Min hors is now so fieble and badde,
And al totore is myn arai,
And every yeer this freisshe Maii
These lusti ladis ryde aboute,
And I mot nedes suie here route
In this manere as ye now se,
And trusse here haltres forth with me,
And am bot as here horse knave.
Non other office I ne have,   1400
Hem thenkth I am worthi nomore,
For I was slow in loves lore,
Whan I was able forto lere,
And wolde noght the tales hiere
Of hem that couthen love teche.'

35

'Now tell me thanne, I you beseche,
Wherof that riche bridel serveth.'
    With that hire chere awei sche swerveth,
And gan to wepe, and thus sche tolde:
'This bridel, which ye nou beholde   1410
So riche upon myn horse hed,—
Ma dame, afore, er I was ded,
Whan I was in mi lusti lif,
Ther fel into myn herte a strif
Of love, which me overcom,
So that therafter hiede I nom
And thoghte I wolde love a kniht:
That laste wel a fourtenyht,
For it no lengere mihte laste,
So nyh my lif was ate laste.   1420
Bot now, allas, to late war
That I ne hadde him loved ar:
For deth cam so in haste bime,
Er I therto hadde eny time,
That it ne mihte ben achieved.
Bot for al that I am relieved,
Of that mi will was good therto,
That love soffreth it be so
That I schal swiche a bridel were.
Now have ye herd al myn ansuere: 1430
To godd, ma dame, I you betake,
And warneth alle for mi sake,
Of love that thei ben noght ydel,
And bidd hem thenke upon mi brydel.'
And with that word al sodeinly
Sche passeth, as it were a sky,
Al clene out of this ladi sihte:
And tho for fere hire herte afflihte,
And seide to hirself, 'Helas!
I am riht in the same cas.   1440
Bot if I live after this day,
I schal amende it, if I may.'
And thus homward this lady wente,

36

And changede al hire ferste entente,
Withinne hire herte and gan to swere
That sche none haltres wolde bere.
  Lo, sone, hier miht thou taken hiede,
How ydelnesse is forto drede,
Namliche of love, as I have write.
For thou miht understonde and wite,   1450
Among the gentil nacion
Love is an occupacion,
Which forto kepe hise lustes save
Scholde every gentil herte have:
For as the ladi was chastised,
Riht so the knyht mai ben avised,
Which ydel is and wol noght serve
To love, he mai per cas deserve
A grettere peine than sche hadde,
Whan sche aboute with hire ladde   1460
The horse haltres; and forthi
Good is to be wel war therbi.
Bot forto loke aboven alle,
These maidens, hou so that it falle,
Thei scholden take ensample of this
Which I have told, for soth it is.
  Mi ladi Venus, whom I serve,
What womman wole hire thonk deserve,
Sche mai noght thilke love eschuie
Of paramours, bot sche mot suie   1470
Cupides lawe; and natheles
Men sen such love sielde in pes,
That it nys evere upon aspie
Of janglinge and of fals Envie,
Fulofte medlid with disese:
Bot thilke love is wel at ese,
Which set is upon mariage;
For that dar schewen the visage
In alle places openly.
A gret mervaile it is forthi,   1480
How that a maiden wolde lette,

37

That sche hir time ne besette
To haste unto that ilke feste,
Wherof the love is al honeste.
Men mai recovere lost of good,
Bot so wys man yit nevere stod,
Which mai recovere time lore:
So mai a maiden wel therfore
Ensample take, of that sche strangeth
Hir love, and longe er that sche changeth   1490
Hir herte upon hir lustes greene
To mariage, as it is seene.
For thus a yer or tuo or thre
Sche lest, er that sche wedded be,
Whyl sche the charge myhte bere
Of children, whiche the world forbere
Ne mai, bot if it scholde faile.
Bot what maiden hire esposaile
Wol tarie, whan sche take mai,
Sche schal per chance an other dai   1500
Be let, whan that hire lievest were.

.   .   .   .

[After telling the tale of Jephthah's daughter the Confessor takes
up the question of love that is won by feats of arms]

That every love of pure kinde
Is ferst forthdrawe, wel I finde:
Bot natheles yit overthis
Decerte doth so that it is
The rather had in mani place.
Forthi who secheth loves grace,   1620
Wher that these worthi wommen are,
He mai noght thanne himselve spare
Upon his travail forto serve,
Wherof that he mai thonk deserve,
There as these men of armes be,
Somtime over the grete se:
So that be londe and ek be schipe
He mot travaile for worschipe

38

And make manye hastyf rodes,
Somtime in Prus, somtime in Rodes,   1630
And somtime into Tartarie;
So that these heraldz on him crie,
'Vailant, vailant, lo, wher he goth!'
And thanne he yifth hem gold and cloth,
So that his fame mihte springe,
And to his ladi ere bringe
Som tidinge of his worthinesse;
So that sche mihte of his prouesce
Of that sche herde men recorde,
The betre unto his love acorde   1640
And danger pute out of hire mod,
Whanne alle men recorden good,
And that sche wot wel, for hir sake
That he no travail wol forsake.
    Mi sone, of this travail I meene:
Nou schrif thee, for it schal be sene
If thou art ydel in this cas.

Amans   My fader ye, and evere was:
For as me thenketh trewely
That every man doth mor than I   1650
As of this point, and if so is
That I have oght so don er this,
It is so litel of acompte,
As who seith, it mai noght amonte
To winne of love his lusti yifte.
For this I telle you in schrifte,
That me were levere hir love winne
Than Kaire and al that is ther inne:
And forto slen the hethen alle,
I not what good ther mihte falle,   1660
So mochel blod thogh ther be schad.
This finde I writen, hou Crist bad
That noman other scholde sle.
What scholde I winne over the se,
If I mi ladi loste at hom?
Bot passe thei the salte fom,

To whom Crist bad thei scholden preche
To al the world and his feith teche:
Bot now thei rucken in here nest
And resten as hem liketh best   1670
In all the swetnesse of delices.
Thus thei defenden ous the vices,
And sitte hemselven al amidde;
To slen and feihten thei ous bidde
Hem whom thei scholde, as the bok seith,
Converten unto Cristes feith.
Bot hierof have I gret mervaile,
Hou thei wol bidde me travaile:
A Sarazin if I sle schal,
I sle the soule forth withal,   1680
And that was nevere Cristes lore.
Bot nou ho ther, I seie nomore.

   Bot I wol speke upon mi schrifte;
And to Cupide I make a yifte,
That who as evere pris deserve
Of armes, I wol love serve;
And thogh I scholde hem bothe kepe,
Als wel yit wolde I take kepe
Whan it were time to abide,
As forto travaile and to ryde: 1690
For how as evere a man laboure,
Cupide appointed hath his houre.

   For I have herd it telle also,
Achilles lefte hise armes so
Bothe of himself and of his men
At Troie for Polixenen,
Upon hire love whanne he fell,
That for no chance that befell
Among the Grecs or up or doun,
He wolde noght ayein the toun   1700
Ben armed, for the love of hire.
And so me thenketh, lieve sire,
A man of armes mai him reste
Somtime in hope for the beste,

If he mai finde a weie nerr.
What scholde I thanne go so ferr
In strange londes many a mile
To ryde, and lese at hom therwhile
Mi love? It were a schort beyete
To winne chaf and lese whete.   1710
Bot if mi ladi bidde wolde,
That I for hire love scholde
Travaile, me thenkth trewely
I mihte fle thurghout the sky,
And go thurghout the depe se,
For al ne sette I at a stre
What thonk that I mihte elles gete.
What helpeth it a man have mete,
Wher drinke lacketh on the bord?
What helpeth eny mannes word   1720
To seie hou I travaile faste,
Wher as me faileth ate laste
That thing which I travaile fore?
O in good time were he bore,
That mihte atteigne such a mede!
Bot certes if I mihte spede
With eny maner besinesse
Of worldes travail, thanne I gesse
Ther scholde me non ydelschipe
Departen fro hir ladischipe.   1730
Bot this I se, on daies nou
The blinde god, I wot noght hou,
Cupido, which of love is lord,
He set the thinges in discord,
That thei that lest to love entende
Fulofte he wole hem yive and sende
Most of his grace; and thus I finde
That he that scholde go behinde,
Goth many a time ferr tofore:
So wot I noght riht wel therfore,   1740
On whether bord that I schal seile.
Thus can I noght miself conseile,

41

Bot al I sette on aventure,
And am, as who seith, out of cure
For ought that I can seie or do:
For everemore I finde it so,
The more besinesse I leie,
The more that I knele and preie
With goode wordes and with softe,
The more I am refused ofte,   1750
With besinesse and mai noght winne.
And in good feith that is gret sinne;
For I mai seie, of dede and thoght
That ydel man have I be noght;
For hou as evere I be deslaied,
Yit evermore I have assaied.
Bot thogh my besinesse laste,
Al is bot ydel ate laste,
For whan th'effect is ydelnesse,
I not what thing is besinesse.   1760
Sei, what availeth al the dede,
Which nothing helpeth ate nede?
For the fortune of every fame
Schal of his ende bere a name.
And thus, for oght is yit befalle,
An ydel man I wol me calle
As after myn entendement:
Bot upon youre amendement,
Min holi fader, as you semeth,
Mi reson and my cause demeth.   1770

V

The lover's wakefulness; the Tale of Ceyx and Alcione;
the prayer of Cephalus (iv. 2771–3258)

Amans   FOR certes, fader Genius,
                     Yit into nou it hath be thus,
                     At alle time if it befelle
                     So that I mihte come and duelle

42

In place ther my ladi were,
I was noght slow ne slepi there:
For thanne I dar wel undertake
That whanne hir list on nyhtes wake
In chambre as to carole and daunce,
Me thenkth I mai me more avaunce, 2780
If I mai gon upon hir hond,
Thanne if I wonne a kinges lond.
For whanne I mai hire hand beclippe,
With such gladnesse I daunce and skippe,
Me thenkth I touche noght the flor;
The ro, which renneth on the mor,
Is thanne noght so lyht as I:
So mow ye witen wel forthi,
That for the time slep I hate.
And whanne it falleth othergate, 2790
So that hire like noght to daunce,
Bot on the dees to caste chaunce
Or axe of love som demande,
Or elles that hir list comaunde
To rede and here of Troilus,
Riht as sche wole or so or thus,
I am al redi to consente.
And if so is that I mai hente
Somtime among a good leisir,
So as I dar of mi desir 2800
I telle a part; bot whanne I preie,
Anon sche bidt me go mi weie
And seith it is ferr in the nyht;
And I swere it is even liht.
Bot as it falleth ate laste,
Ther mai no worldes joie laste,
So mot I nedes fro hire wende
And of my wachche make an ende:
And if sche thanne hiede toke,
Hou pitousliche on hire I loke, 2810
Whan that I schal my leve take,
Hire oghte of mercy forto slake

43

Hire daunger, which seith evere nay.
    Bot he seith often, 'Have good day,'
That loth is forto take his leve:
Therfore, while I mai beleve,
I tarie forth the nyht along,
For it is noght on me along
To slep that I so sone go,
Til that I mot algate so;   2820
And thanne I bidde godd hire se,
And so doun knelende on mi kne
I take leve, and if I schal,
I kisse hire, and go forth withal.
And otherwhile, if that I dore,
Er I come fulli to the dore,
I torne ayein and feigne a thing,
As thogh I hadde lost a ring
Or somwhat elles, for I wolde
Kisse hire eftsones, if I scholde,   2830
Bot selden is that I so spede.
And whanne I se that I mot nede
Departen, I departe, and thanne
With al myn herte I curse and banne
That evere slep was mad for yhe;
For, as me thenkth, I mihte dryhe
Withoute slep to waken evere,
So that I scholde noght dissevere
Fro hire, in whom is al my liht:
And thanne I curse also the nyht   2840
With al the will of mi corage,
And seie, 'Awey, thou blake ymage,
Which of thi derke cloudy face
Makst al the worldes lyht deface,
And causest unto slep a weie,
Be which I mot nou gon aweie
Out of mi ladi compaignie.
O slepi nyht, I thee defie,
And wolde that thou leye in presse
With Proserpine the goddesse   2850

44

And with Pluto the helle king:
For til I se the daies spring,
I sette slep noght at a risshe.'
And with that word I sike and wisshe,
And seie, 'Ha, whi ne were it day?
For yit mi ladi thanne I may
Beholde, thogh I do nomore.'
And efte I thenke forthermore,
To som man hou the niht doth ese,
Whan he hath thing that mai him plese   2860
The longe nyhtes be his side,
Where as I faile and go beside.
Bot slep, I not wherof it serveth,
Of which noman his thonk deserveth
To gete him love in eny place,
Bot is an hindrere of his grace
And makth him ded as for a throwe,
Riht as a stok were overthrowe.
And so, mi fader, in this wise
The slepi nyhtes I despise,   2870
And evere amiddes of mi tale
I thenke upon the nyhtingale,
Which slepeth noght be weie of kinde
For love, in bokes as I finde.
Thus ate laste I go to bedde,
And yit min herte lith to wedde
With hire, wher as I cam fro;
Thogh I departe, he wol noght so,
Ther is no lock mai schette him oute,
Him nedeth noght to gon aboute,   2880
That perce mai the harde wall;
Thus is he with hire overall,
That be hire lief, or be hire loth,
Into hire bedd myn herte goth,
And softly takth hire in his arm
And fieleth hou that sche is warm,
And wissheth that his body were
To fiele that he fieleth there.

And thus miselven I tormente,
Til that the dede slep me hente: 2890
Bot thanne be a thousand score
Welmore than I was tofore
I am tormented in mi slep,
Bot that I dreme is noght of schep;
For I ne thenke noght on wulle,
Bot I am drecched to the fulle
Of love, that I have to kepe,
That nou I lawhe and nou I wepe,
And nou I lese and nou I winne,
And nou I ende and nou beginne.   2900
And otherwhile I dreme and mete
That I al one with hire mete
And that Danger is left behinde;
And thanne in slep such joie I finde,
That I ne bede nevere awake.
Bot after, whanne I hiede take,
And schal arise upon the morwe,
Thanne is al torned into sorwe,
Noght for the cause I schal arise,
Bot for I mette in such a wise,   2910
And ate laste I am bethoght
That al is vein and helpeth noght:
Bot yit me thenketh be my wille
I wolde have leie and slepe stille,
To meten evere of such a swevene,
For thanne I hadde a slepi hevene.

Mi sone, and for thou tellest so,
A man mai finde of time ago
That many a swevene hath be certein,
Al be it so, that som men sein   2920
That swevenes ben of no credence.
Bot forto schewe in evidence
That thei fulofte sothe thinges
Betokne, I thenke in my wrytinges
To telle a tale therupon,
Which fell be olde daies gon.

46

This finde I write in Poesie:
Ceïx the king of Trocinie
Hadde Alceone to his wif,
Which as hire oghne hertes lif   2930
Him loveth; and he hadde also
A brother, which was cleped tho
Dedalion, and he per cas
Fro kinde of man forschape was
Into a goshauk of liknesse;
Wherof the king gret hevynesse
Hath take, and thoghte in his corage
To gon upon a pelrinage
Into a strange regioun,
Wher he hath his devocioun   2940
To don his sacrifice and preie,
If that he mihte in eny weie
Toward the goddes finde grace
His brother hele to pourchace,
So that he mihte be reformed
Of that he hadde be transformed.
To this pourpos and to this ende
This king is redy forto wende,
As he which wolde go be schipe;
And forto don him felaschipe   2950
His wif unto the see him broghte,
With al hire herte and him besoghte,
That he the time hire wolde sein,
Whan that he thoghte come ayein:
'Withinne,' he seith, 'tuo monthe day.'
And thus in al the haste he may
He tok his leve, and forth he seileth,
Wepende and sche hirself beweileth,
And torneth hom, ther sche cam fro.
Bot whan the monthes were ago,   2960
The whiche he sette of his comynge,
And that sche herde no tydinge,
Ther was no care forto seche:
Wherof the goddes to beseche

47

Tho sche began in many wise,
And to Juno hire sacrifise
Above alle othre most sche dede,
And for hir lord sche hath so bede
To wite and knowe hou that he ferde,
That Juno the goddesse hire herde,   2970
Anon and upon this matiere
Sche bad Yris hir messagere
To Slepes hous that sche schal wende,
And bidde him that he make an ende
Be swevene and schewen al the cas
Unto this ladi, hou it was.

  This Yris, fro the hihe stage
Which undertake hath the message,
Hire reyny cope dede upon,
The which was wonderli begon   2980
With colours of diverse hewe,
An hundred mo than men it knewe;
The hevene lich unto a bowe
Sche bende, and so she cam doun lowe,
The god of Slep wher that sche fond.
And that was in a strange lond,
Which marcheth upon Chymerie:
For ther, as seith the Poesie,
The god of Slep hath mad his hous,
Which of entaille is merveilous.   2990
Under an hell ther is a cave,
Which of the sonne mai noght have,
So that noman mai knowe ariht
The point betwen the dai and nyht:
Ther is no fyr, ther is no sparke,
Ther is no dore, which mai charke,
Wherof an yhe scholde unschette,
So that inward ther is no lette.
And forto speke of that withoute,
Ther stant no gret tree nyh aboute   3000
Wher on ther myhte crowe or pie
Alihte, forto clepe or crie:

Ther is no cok to crowe day,
Ne beste non which noise may;
The hell bot al aboute round
Ther is growende upon the ground
Popi, which berth the sed of slep,
With othre herbes suche an hep.
A stille water for the nones
Rennende upon the smale stones,   3010
Which hihte of Lethes the rivere,
Under that hell in such manere
Ther is, which yifth gret appetit
To slepe. And thus full of delit
Slep hath his hous; and of his couche
Withinne his chambre if I schal touche,
Of hebenus that slepi tree
The bordes al aboute be,
And for he scholde slepe softe,
Upon a fethrebed alofte   3020
He lith with many a pilwe of doun:
The chambre is strowed up and doun
With swevenes many thousendfold.
Thus cam Yris into this hold,
And to the bedd, which is al blak,
Sche goth, and ther with Slep sche spak,
And in the wise as sche was bede
The message of Juno sche dede.
Fulofte hir wordes sche reherceth,
Er sche his slepi eres perceth;   3030
With mochel wo bot ate laste
His slombrende yhen he upcaste
And seide hir that it schal be do.
Wherof among a thousend tho,
Withinne his hous that slepi were,
In special he ches out there
Thre, whiche scholden do this dede:
The ferste of hem, so as I rede,
Was Morpheüs, the whos nature
Is forto take the figure   3040

Of what persone that him liketh,
Wherof that he fulofte entriketh
The lif which slepe schal be nyhte;
And Ithecus that other hihte,
Which hath the vois of every soun,
The chiere and the condicioun
Of every lif, what so it is:
The thridde suiende after this
Is Panthasas, which may transforme
Of every thing the rihte forme,   3050
And change it in an other kinde.
Upon hem thre, so as I finde,
Of swevencs stant al th'apparence,
Which otherwhile is evidence
And otherwhile bot a jape.
Bot natheles it is so schape,
That Morpheüs be nyht al one
Appiereth until Alceone
In liknesse of hir housebonde
Al naked ded upon the stronde,   3060
And hou he dreynte in special
These othre tuo it schewen al.
The tempeste of the blake cloude,
The wode see, the wyndes loude,
Al this sche mette, and sih him dyen;
Wherof that sche began to crien,
Slepende abedde ther sche lay,
And with that noise of hire affray
Hir wommen sterten up aboute,
Whiche of here ladi were in doute,   3070
And axen hire hou that sche ferde;
And sche, riht as sche syh and herde,
Hir swevene hath told hem everydel.
And thei it halsen alle wel
And sein it is a tokne of goode;
Bot til sche wiste hou that it stode,
Sche hath no confort in hire herte,
Upon the morwe and up sche sterte,

And to the see, wher that sche mette
The bodi lay, withoute lette   3080
Sche drowh, and whan that sche cam nyh,
Stark ded, hise armes sprad, sche syh
Hire lord flietende upon the wawe.
Wherof hire wittes ben withdrawe,
And sche, which tok of deth no kepe,
Anon forth lepte into the depe
And wolde have cawht him in hire arm.
  This infortune of double harm
The goddes fro the hevene above
Behielde, and for the trowthe of love,   3090
Which in this worthi ladi stod,
Thei have upon the salte flod
Hire dreinte lord and hire also
Fro deth to lyve torned so,
That thei ben schapen into briddes
Swimmende upon the wawe amiddes.
And whan sche sih hire lord livende
In liknesse of a bridd swimmende,
And sche was of the same sort,
So as sche mihte do desport,   3100
Upon the joie which sche hadde
Hire wynges bothe abrod sche spradde,
And him, so as sche mai suffise,
Beclipte and keste in such a wise,
As sche was whilom wont to do:
Hire wynges for hire armes tuo
Sche tok, and for hire lippes softe
Hire harde bile, and so fulofte
Sche fondeth in hire briddes forme,
If that sche mihte hirself conforme   3110
To do the plesance of a wif,
As sche dede in that other lif:
For thogh sche hadde hir pouer lore,
Hir will stod as it was tofore,
And serveth him so as sche mai.
Wherof into this ilke day

Togedre upon the see thei wone,
Wher many a dowhter and a Sone
Thei bringen forth of briddes kinde;
And for men scholden take in mynde   3120
This Alceoun the trewe queene,
Hire briddes yit, as it is seene,
Of Alceoun the name bere.

Confessor

    Lo thus, mi sone, it mai thee stere
Of swevenes forto take kepe,
For ofte time a man aslepe
Mai se what after schal betide.
Forthi it helpeth at som tyde
A man to slepe, as it belongeth,
Bot Slowthe no lif underfongeth   3130
Which is to love appourtenant.

Amans

    Mi fader, upon covenant
I dar wel make this avou,
Of all mi lif that into nou,
Als fer as I can understonde,
Yit tok I nevere slep on honde,
Whan it was time forto wake;
For thogh myn yhe it wolde take,
Min herte is evere therayein.
Bot natheles to speke it plein,   3140
Al this that I have seid you hiere
Of my wakinge, as ye mai hiere,
It toucheth to mi lady swete;
For otherwise, I you behiete,
In strange place whanne I go,
Me list nothing to wake so.
For whan the wommen listen pleie,
And I hir se noght in the weie,
Of whom I scholde merthe take,
Me list noght longe forto wake,   3150
Bot if it be for pure schame,
Of that I wolde eschuie a name,
That thei ne scholde have cause non
To seie, 'Ha, lo, wher goth such on,

That hath forlore his contenaunce!'
And thus among I singe and daunce,
And feigne lust ther as non is.
For ofte sithe I fiele this;
Of thoght, which in mi herte falleth
Whanne it is nyht, myn hed appalleth,   3160
And that is for I se hire noght,
Which is the wakere of mi thoght:
And thus as tymliche as I may,
Fulofte whanne it is brod day,
I take of all these othre leve
And go my weie, and thei beleve,
That sen per cas here loves there;
And I go forth as noght ne were
Unto mi bedd, so that al one
I mai ther ligge and sighe and grone   3170
And wisshen al the longe nyht,
Til that I se the daies lyht.
I not if that be Sompnolence,
Bot upon youre conscience,
Min holi fader, demeth ye.

Confessor   My sone, I am wel paid with thee,
Of Slep that thou the Sluggardie
Be nyhte in loves compaignie
Eschuied hast, and do thi peine
So that thi love thar noght pleine: 3180
For love upon his lust wakende
Is evere, and wolde that non ende
Were of the longe nyhtes set.
Wherof that thou be war the bet,
To telle a tale I am bethoght,
Hou love and Slep acorden noght.

For love who that list to wake
Be nyhte, he mai ensample take
Of Cephalus, whan that he lay
With Aurora that swete may   3190
In armes all the longe nyht.

53

Bot whanne it drogh toward the liht,
That he withinne his herte sih
The dai which was amorwe nyh,
Anon unto the Sonne he preide
For lust of love, and thus he seide:
  'O Phebus, which the daies liht
Governest, til that it be nyht,
And gladest every creature
After the lawe of thi nature,—   3200
Bot natheles ther is a thing,
Which onli to the knouleching
Belongeth as in privete
To love and to his duete,
Which asketh noght to ben apert,
Bot in cilence and in covert
Desireth forto be beschaded:
And thus whan that thi liht is faded
And Vesper scheweth him alofte,
And that the nyht is long and softe,   3210
Under the cloudes derke and stille
Thanne hath this thing most of his wille.
Forthi unto thi myhtes hyhe,
As thou which art the daies yhe,
Of love and myht no conseil hyde,
Upon this derke nyhtes tyde
With al myn herte I thee beseche
That I plesance myhte seche
With hire which lith in min armes.
Withdrawgh the banere of thin armes, 3220
And let thi lyhtes ben unborn,
And in the signe of Capricorn,
The hous appropred to Satorne,
I preie that thou wolt sojorne,
Wher ben the nihtes derke and longe:
For I mi love have underfonge,
Which lith hier be mi syde naked,
As sche which wolde ben awaked,
And me lest nothing forto slepe.

So were it good to take kepe   3230
Nou at this nede of mi preiere,
And that the like forto stiere
Thi fyri carte, and so ordeigne
That thou thi swifte hors restreigne
Lowe under erthe in Occident,
That thei towardes Orient
Be cercle go the longe weie.
  And ek to thee, Diane, I preie,
Which cleped art of thi noblesse
The nyhtes mone and the goddesse,   3240
That thou to me be gracious:
And in Cancro thin oghne hous
Ayein Phebus in opposit
Stond al this time, and of delit
Behold Venus with a glad yhe.
For thanne upon astronomie
Of due constellacion
Thou makst prolificacion,
And dost that children ben begete:
Which grace if that I mihte gete,   3250
With al myn herte I wolde serve
Be nyhte, and thi vigile observe.'
  Lo, thus this lusti Cephalus
Preide unto Phebe and to Phebus
The nyht in lengthe forto drawe,
So that he mihte do the lawe
In thilke point of loves heste,
Which cleped is the nyhtes fest. . . .

VI

The Tale of Jason and Medea (v. 3247–4174)

IN Grece whilom was a king,
Of whom the fame and knowleching
Beleveth yit, and Peleïs
He hihte; bot it fell him thus,   3250

55

That his fortune hir whiel so ladde
That he no child his oghne hadde
To regnen after his decess.
He hadde a brother natheles,
Whos rihte name was Eson,
And he the worthi kniht Jason
Begat, the which in every lond
Alle othre passede of his hond
In armes, so that he the beste
Was named and the worthieste, 3260
He soghte worschipe overal.
Nou herkne, and I thee telle schal
An aventure that he soghte,
Which afterward ful dere he boghte.
    Ther was an yle, which Colchos
Was cleped, and therof aros
Gret speche in every lond aboute,
That such merveile was non oute
In al the wyde world nawhere,
As tho was in that yle there. 3270
Ther was a schiep, as it was told,
The which his flees bar al of gold,
And so the goddes hadde it set,
That it ne mihte awei be fet
Be pouer of no worldes wiht:
And yit ful many a worthi kniht
It hadde assaied, as thei dorste,
And evere it fell hem to the worste.
Bot he, that wolde it noght forsake,
Bot of his knyhthod undertake 3280
To do what thing therto belongeth,
This worthi Jason, sore alongeth
To se the strange regiouns
And knowe the condiciouns
Of othre marches, where he wente;
And for that cause his hole entente
He sette Colchos forto seche,
And therupon he made a speche

To Peleüs his em the king.
And he wel paid was of that thing;   3290
And schop anon for his passage,
And suche as were of his lignage,
With othre knihtes whiche he ches,
With him he tok, and Hercules,
Which full was of chivalerie,
With Jason wente in compaignie;
And that was in the monthe of Maii,
Whan colde stormes were away.
The wynd was good, the chip was yare,
Thei tok here leve, and forth thei fare   3300
Toward Colchos: bot on the weie
What hem befell is long to seie;
Hou Lamedon the king of Troie,
Which oghte wel have mad hem joie,
Whan thei to reste a while him preide,
Out of his lond he hem congeide;
And so fell the dissencion,
Which after was destruccion
Of that cite, as men mai hiere:
Bot that is noght to mi matiere.   3310
Bot thus this worthi folk Gregeis
Fro that king, which was noght curteis,
And fro his lond with sail updrawe
Thei wente hem forth, and many a sawe
Thei made and many a gret manace,
Til ate laste into that place
Which as thei soghte thei aryve,
And striken sail, and forth as blyve
Thei sente unto the king and tolden
Who weren ther and what thei wolden.   3320
Oëtes, which was thanne king,
Whan that he herde this tyding
Of Jason, which was comen there,
And of these othre, what thei were,
He thoghte don hem gret worschipe:
For thei anon come out of schipe,

And strawht unto the king thei wente,
And be the hond Jason he hente,
And that was ate paleis gate,
So fer the king cam on his gate 3330
Toward Jason to don him chiere;
And he, whom lacketh no manere,
Whan he the king sih in presence,
Yaf him ayein such reverence
As to a kinges stat belongeth.
And thus the king him underfongeth,
And Jason in his arm he cawhte,
And forth into the halle he strawhte,
And ther they siete and spieke of thinges,
And Jason tolde him tho tidinges, 3340
Why he was come, and faire him preide
To haste his time, and the kyng seide,
'Jason, thou art a worthi kniht,
Bot it lith in no mannes myht
To don that thou art come fore:
Ther hath be many a kniht forlore
Of that thei wolden it assaie.'
Bot Jason wolde him noght esmaie,
And seide, 'Of every worldes cure
Fortune stant in aventure, 3350
Per aunter wel, per aunter wo:
Bot hou as evere that it go,
It schal be with myn hond assaied.'
The king tho hield him noght wel paied,
For he the Grekes sore dredde,
In aunter, if Jason ne spedde,
He mihte therof bere a blame;
For tho was al the worldes fame
In Grece, as forto speke of armes.
Forthi he dredde him of his harmes, 3360
And gan to preche him and to preie;
Bot Jason wolde noght obeie,
Bot seide he wolde his porpos holde
For ought that eny man him tolde.

The king, whan he thes wordes herde,
And sih hou that this kniht ansuerde,
Yit for he wolde make him glad,
After Medea gon he bad,
Which was his dowhter, and sche cam.
And Jason, which good hiede nam,   3370
Whan he hire sih, ayein hire goth;
And sche, which was him nothing loth,
Welcomede him into that lond,
And softe tok him be the hond,
And doun thei seten bothe same.
Sche hadde herd spoke of his name
And of his grete worthinesse;
Forthi sche gan hir yhe impresse
Upon his face and his stature,
And thoghte hou nevere creature   3380
Was so wel farende as was he.
And Jason riht in such degre
Ne mihte noght withholde his lok,
Bot so good hiede on hire he tok,
That him ne thoghte under the hevene
Of beaute sawh he nevere hir evene,
With al that fell to wommanhiede.
Thus ech of other token hiede,
Thogh ther no word was of record;
Here hertes bothe of on acord   3390
Ben set to love, bot as tho
Ther mihten be no wordes mo.
The king made him gret joie and feste,
To alle his men he yaf an heste,
So as thei wolde his thonk deserve,
That thei scholde alle Jason serve,
Whil that he wolde there duelle.
And thus the dai, shortly to telle,
With manye merthes thei despente,
Til nyht was come, and tho thei wente,   3400
Echon of other tok his leve,
Whan thei no lengere myhten leve.

I not hou Jason that nyht slep,
Bot wel I wot that of the schep,
For which he cam into that yle,
He thoghte bot a litel whyle;
Al was Medea that he thoghte,
So that in many a wise he soghte
His witt wakende er it was day,
Som time yee, som time nay,   3410
Som time thus, som time so,
As he was stered to and fro
Of love, and ek of his conqueste
As he was holde of his beheste.
And thus he ros up be the morwe
And tok himself seint John to borwe,
And seide he wolde ferst beginne
At love, and after forto winne
The flees of gold, for which he com,
And thus to him good herte he nom.   3420
    Medea riht the same wise,
Til dai cam that sche moste arise,
Lay and bethoughte hire al the nyht,
Hou sche that noble worthi kniht
Be eny weie mihte wedde:
And wel sche wiste, if he ne spedde
Of thing which he hadde undertake,
Sche mihte hirself no porpos take;
For if he deide of his bataile,
Sche moste thanne algate faile   3430
To geten him, whan he were ded.
Thus sche began to sette red
And torne about hir wittes alle,
To loke hou that it mihte falle
That sche with him hadde a leisir
To speke and telle of hir desir.
And so it fell that same day
That Jason with that suete may
Togedre sete and hadden space
To speke, and he besoughte hir grace.   3440

And sche his tale goodli herde,
And afterward sche him ansuerde
And seide, 'Jason, as thou wilt,
Thou miht be sauf, thou miht be spilt;
For wite wel that nevere man,
Bot if he couthe that I can,
Ne mihte that fortune achieve
For which thou comst: bot as I lieve,
If thou wolt holde covenant
To love, of al the remenant   3450
I schal thi lif and honour save,
That thou the flees of gold schalt have.'
He seide, 'Al at youre oghne wille,
Ma dame, I schal treuly fulfille
Youre heste, whil mi lif mai laste.'
Thus longe he preide, and ate laste
Sche granteth, and behihte him this,
That whan nyht comth and it time is,
Sche wolde him sende certeinly
Such on that scholde him prively   3460
Al one into hire chambre bringe.
He thonketh hire of that tidinge,
For of that grace him is begonne
Him thenkth alle othre thinges wonne.

    The dai made ende and lost his lyht,
And comen was the derke nyht,
Which al the daies yhe blente.
Jason tok leve and forth he wente,
And whan he cam out of the pres,
He tok to conseil Hercules,   3470
And tolde him hou it was betid,
And preide it scholde wel ben hid,
And that he wolde loke aboute,
Therwhiles that he schal ben oute.
Thus as he stod and hiede nam,
A mayden fro Medea cam
And to hir chambre Jason ledde,
Wher that he fond redi to bedde

The faireste and the wiseste eke;
And sche with simple chiere and meke,   3480
Whan sche him sih, wax al aschamed.
Tho was here tale newe entamed;
For sikernesse of mariage
Sche fette forth a riche ymage,
Which was figure of Jupiter,
And Jason swor and seide ther,
That also wiss god scholde him helpe,
That if Medea dede him helpe,
That he his pourpos myhte winne,
Thei scholde nevere parte atwinne,   3490
Bot evere whil him lasteth lif,
He wolde hire holde for his wif.
And with that word thei kisten bothe;
And for thei scholden hem unclothe,
Ther cam a maide, and in hir wise
Sche dede hem bothe full servise,
Til that thei were in bedde naked:
I wot that nyht was wel bewaked,
Thei hadden bothe what thei wolde.
And thanne of leisir sche him tolde,   3500
And gan fro point to point enforme
Of his bataile and al the forme,
Which as he scholde finde there,
Whan he to th'yle come were.
     Sche seide, at entre of the pas
Hou Mars, which god of armes was,
Hath set tuo Oxen sterne and stoute,
That caste fyr and flamme aboute
Bothe at the mouth and ate nase,
So that thei setten al on blase   3510
What thing that passeth hem betwene:
And forthermore upon the grene
Ther goth the flees of gold to kepe
A serpent, which mai nevere slepe.
Thus who that evere scholde it winne,
The fyr to stoppe he mot beginne,

Which that the fierce bestes caste,
And daunte he mot hem ate laste,
So that he mai hem yoke and dryve;
And therupon he mot as blyve   3520
The serpent with such strengthe assaile,
That he mai slen him be bataile;
Of which he mot the teth outdrawe,
As it belongeth to that lawe,
And thanne he mot tho oxen yoke,
Til thei have with a plowh tobroke
A furgh of lond, in which arowe
The teth of thaddre he moste sowe,
And therof schule arise knihtes
Wel armed up at alle rihtes.   3530
Of hem is noght to taken hiede,
For ech of hem in hastihiede
Schal other slen with dethes wounde:
And thus whan thei ben leid to grounde,
Than mot he to the goddes preie,
And go so forth and take his preie.
Bot if he faile in eny wise
Of that ye hiere me devise,
Ther mai be set non other weie,
That he ne moste algates deie.   3540
'Nou have I told the peril al:
I woll you tellen forth withal,'
Quod Medea to Jason tho,
'That ye schul knowen er ye go,
Ayein the venym and the fyr
What schal ben the recoverir.
Bot, sire, for it is nyh day,
Ariseth up, so that I may
Delivere you what thing I have,
That mai youre lif and honour save.'   3550
Thei weren bothe loth to rise,
Bot for thei weren bothe wise,
Up thei arisen ate laste:
Jason his clothes on him caste

And made him redi riht anon,
And sche hir scherte dede upon
And caste on hire a mantel clos,
Withoute more and thanne aros.
Tho tok sche forth a riche tye
Mad al of gold and of perrie, 3560
Out of the which sche nam a ring,
The ston was worth al other thing.
Sche seide, whil he wolde it were,
Ther myhte no peril him dere,
In water mai it noght be dreynt,
Wher as it comth the fyr is queynt,
It daunteth ek the cruel beste,
Ther may no qued that man areste,
Wher so he be on see or lond,
Which hath that ring upon his hond: 3570
And over that sche gan to sein,
That if a man wol ben unsein,
Withinne his hond hold clos the ston,
And he mai invisible gon.
The ring to Jason sche betauhte,
And so forth after sche him tauhte
What sacrifise he scholde make;
And gan out of hire cofre take
Him thoughte an hevenely figure,
Which al be charme and be conjure 3580
Was wroght, and ek it was thurgh write
With names, which he scholde wite,
As sche him tauhte tho to rede;
And bad him, as he wolde spede,
Withoute reste of eny while,
Whan he were londed in that yle,
He scholde make his sacrifise
And rede his carecte in the wise
As sche him tauhte, on knes doun bent,
Thre sithes toward Orient; 3590
For so scholde he the goddes plese
And winne himselven mochel ese.

And whanne he hadde it thries rad,
To opne a buiste sche him bad,
Which sche ther tok him in present,
And was full of such oignement,
That ther was fyr ne venym non
That scholde fastnen him upon,
Whan that he were enoynt withal.
Forthi sche tauhte him hou he schal   3600
Enoignte his armes al aboute,
And for he scholde nothing doute,
Sche tok him thanne a maner glu,
The which was of so gret vertu,
That where a man it wolde caste,
It scholde binde anon so faste
That noman mihte it don aweie.
And that sche bad be alle weie
He scholde into the mouthes throwen
Of tho tweie oxen that fyr blowen,   3610
Therof to stoppen the malice;
The glu schal serve of that office.
And over that hir oignement,
Hir ring and hir enchantement
Ayein the serpent scholde him were,
Til he him sle with swerd or spere:
And thanne he may saufliche ynowh
His oxen yoke into the plowh
And the teth sowe in such a wise,
Til he the knyhtes se arise,   3620
And ech of other doun be leid
In such manere as I have seid.
    Lo, thus Medea for Jason
Ordeigneth, and preith therupon
That he nothing foryete scholde,
And ek sche preith him that he wolde,
Whan he hath alle his armes don,
To grounde knele and thonke anon
The goddes, and so forth be ese
The flees of gold he scholde sese.   3630

And whanne he hadde it sesed so,
That thanne he were sone ago
Withouten eny tariynge.
　Whan this was seid, into wepinge
Sche fell, as sche that was thurgh nome
With love, and so fer overcome,
That al hir world on him sche sette.
Bot whan sche sih ther was no lette,
That he mot nedes parte hire fro,
Sche tok him in hire armes tuo,　　　　　　　3640
An hundred time and gan him kisse,
And seide, 'O, al mi worldes blisse,
Mi trust, mi lust, mi lif, min hele,
To be thin helpe in this querele
I preie unto the goddes alle.'
And with that word sche gan doun falle
On swoune, and he hire uppe nam,
And forth with that the maiden cam,
And thei to bedde anon hir broghte,
And thanne Jason hire besoghte,　　　　　　　3650
And to hire seide in this manere:
'Mi worthi lusti ladi dere,
Conforteth you, for be my trouthe
It schal noght fallen in mi slouthe
That I ne wol thurghout fulfille
Youre hestes at youre oghne wille.
And yit I hope to you bringe
Withinne a while such tidinge,
The which schal make ous bothe game.'
　Bot for he wolde kepe hir name,　　　　　　　3660
Whan that he wiste it was nyh dai,
He seide, 'A dieu, mi swete mai.'
And forth with him he nam his gere,
Which as sche hadde take him there,
And strauht unto his chambre he wente,
And goth to bedde and slep him hente,
And lay, that noman him awok,
For Hercules hiede of him tok,

Til it was undren hih and more.
And thanne he gan to sighe sore   3670
And sodeinliche abreide of slep;
And thei that token of him kep,
His chamberleins, be sone there,
And maden redi al his gere,
And he aros and to the king
He wente, and seide hou to that thing
For which he cam he wolde go.
The king therof was wonder wo,
And for he wolde him fain withdrawe,
He tolde him many a dredful sawe,   3680
Bot Jason wolde it noght recorde,
And ate laste thei acorde.
Whan that he wolde noght abide,
A bot was redy ate tyde,
In which this worthi kniht of Grece
Ful armed up at every piece,
To his bataile which belongeth,
Tok ore on honde and sore him longeth,
Til he the water passed were.
    Whan he cam to that yle there,   3690
He set him on his knes doun strauht,
And his carecte, as he was tawht,
He radde, and made his sacrifise,
And siththe enoignte him in that wise,
As Medea him hadde bede;
And thanne aros up fro that stede,
And with the glu the fyr he queynte,
And anon after he atteinte
The grete serpent and him slowh.
Bot erst he hadde sorwe ynowh,   3700
For that serpent made him travaile
So harde and sore of his bataile,
That nou he stod and nou he fell:
For longe time it so befell,
That with his swerd ne with his spere
He mihte noght that serpent dere.

67

He was so scherded al aboute,
It hield all eggetol withoute,
He was so ruide and hard of skin,
Ther mihte nothing go therin;   3710
Venym and fyr togedre he caste,
That he Jason so sore ablaste,
That if ne were his oignement,
His ring and his enchantement,
Which Medea tok him tofore,
He hadde with that worm be lore;
Bot of vertu which therof cam
Jason the dragon overcam.
And he anon the teth outdrouh,
And sette his oxen in a plouh,   3720
With which he brak a piece of lond
And sieu hem with his oghne hond.
Tho mihte he gret merveile se:
Of every toth in his degre
Sprong up a kniht with spere and schield,
Of whiche anon riht in the field
Echon slow other; and with that
Jason Medea noght foryat,
On bothe his knes he gan doun falle,
And yaf thonk to the goddes alle.   3730
The flees he tok and goth to bote,
The sonne schyneth bryhte and hote,
The flees of gold schon forth withal,
The water glistreth overal.
  Medea wepte and sigheth ofte,
And stod upon a tour alofte:
Al prively withinne hirselve,
Ther herde it nouther ten ne tuelve,
Sche preide, and seide, 'O, god him spede,
The kniht which hath mi maidenhiede!'   3740
And ay sche loketh toward th'yle.
Bot whan sche sih withinne a while
The flees glistrende ayein the sonne,
Sche saide, 'Ha lord, now al is wonne,

Mi kniht the field hath overcome:
Nou wolde god he were come;
Ha lord, that he ne were alonde!'
Bot I dar take this on honde,
If that sche hadde wynges tuo,
Sche wolde have flowe unto him tho   3750
Strawht ther he was into the bot.
   The dai was clier, the sonne hot,
The Gregeis weren in gret doute,
The whyle that here lord was oute:
Thei wisten noght what scholde tyde,
Bot waiten evere upon the tyde,
To se what ende scholde falle.
Ther stoden ek the nobles alle
Forth with the comun of the toun;
And as thei loken up and doun,   3760
Thei weren war withinne a throwe,
Wher cam the bot, which thei wel knowe,
And sihe hou Jason broghte his preie.
And tho thei gonnen alle seie,
And criden alle with o stevene,
'Ha, wher was evere under the hevene
So noble a knyht as Jason is?'
And welnyh alle seiden this,
That Jason was a faie kniht,
For it was nevere of mannes miht   3770
The flees of gold so forto winne;
And thus to talen thei beginne.
With that the king com forth anon,
And sih the flees, hou that it schon;
And whan Jason cam to the lond,
The king himselve tok his hond
And kist him, and gret joie him made.
The Gregeis weren wonder glade,
And of that thing riht merie hem thoghte,
And forth with hem the flees thei broghte,   3780
And ech on other gan to leyhe;
Bot wel was him that mihte neyhe,

To se therof the proprete.
And thus thei passen the cite
And gon unto the paleis straght.
　Medea, which foryat him naght,
Was redy there, and seide anon,
'Welcome, O worthi kniht Jason.'
Sche wolde have kist him wonder fayn,
Bot schame tornede hire agayn; 3790
It was noght the manere as tho,
Forthi sche dorste noght do so.
Sche tok hire leve, and Jason wente
Into his chambre, and sche him sente
Hire maide to sen hou he ferde;
The which whan that sche sih and herde,
Hou that he hadde faren oute
And that it stod wel al aboute,
Sche tolde hire ladi what sche wiste,
And sche for joie hire maide kiste. 3800
The bathes weren thanne araied,
With herbes tempred and assaied,
And Jason was unarmed sone
And dede as it befell to done:
Into his bath he wente anon
And wyssh him clene as eny bon;
He tok a sopp, and oute he cam,
And on his beste aray he nam,
And kempde his hed, whan he was clad,
And goth him forth al merie and glad 3810
Riht strawht into the kinges halle.
The king cam with his knihtes alle
And maden him glad welcominge;
And he hem tolde the tidinge
Of this and that, hou it befell,
Whan that he wan the schepes fell.
　Medea, whan sche was asent,
Com sone to that parlement,
And whan sche mihte Jason se,
Was non so glad of alle as sche. 3820

Ther was no joie forto seche,
Of him mad every man a speche,
Som man seide on, som man seide other;
Bot thogh he were goddes brother
And mihte make fyr and thonder,
Ther mihte be nomore wonder
Than was of him in that cite.
Echon tauhte other, 'This is he,
Which hath in his pouer withinne
That al the world ne mihte winne: 3830
Lo, hier the beste of alle goode.'
Thus saiden thei that there stode,
And ek that walkede up and doun,
Bothe of the court and of the toun.
    The time of souper cam anon,
Thei wisshen and therto thei gon,
Medea was with Jason set:
Tho was ther many a deynte fet
And set tofore hem on the bord,
Bot non so likinge as the word   3840
Which was ther spoke among hem tuo,
So as thei dorste speke tho.
Bot thogh thei hadden litel space,
Yit thei acorden in that place
Hou Jason scholde come at nyht,
Whan every torche and every liht
Were oute, and thanne of other thinges
Thei spieke aloud for supposinges
Of hem that stoden there aboute:
For love is everemore in doute,   3850
If that it be wisly governed
Of hem that ben of love lerned.
    Whan al was don, that dissh and cuppe
And cloth and bord and al was uppe,
Thei waken whil hem lest to wake,
And after that thei leve take
And gon to bedde forto reste.
And whan him thoghte for the beste,

That every man was faste aslepe,
Jason, that wolde his time kepe,   3860
Goth forth stalkende al prively
Unto the chambre, and redely
Ther was a maide, which him kepte.
Medea wok and nothing slepte,
Bot natheles sche was abedde,
And he with alle haste him spedde
And made him naked and al warm.
Anon he tok hire in his arm:
What nede is forto speke of ese?
Hem list ech other forto plese,   3870
So that thei hadden joie ynow:
And tho thei setten whanne and how
That sche with him awey schal stele.
With wordes suche and othre fele
Whan al was treted to an ende,
Jason tok leve and gan forth wende
Unto his oughne chambre in pes;
Ther wiste it non bot Hercules.

   He slepte and ros whan it was time,
And whanne it fell towardes prime,   3880
He tok to him suche as he triste
In secre, that non other wiste,
And told hem of his conseil there,
And seide that his wille were
That thei to schipe hadde alle thinge
So priveliche in th'evenynge,
That noman mihte here dede aspie
Bot tho that were of compaignie:
For he woll go withoute leve,
And lengere woll he noght beleve;   3890
Bot he ne wolde at thilke throwe
The king or queene scholde it knowe.
Thei saide, 'Al this schal wel be do:'
And Jason truste wel therto.
   Medea in the mene while,
Which thoghte hir fader to beguile,

The tresor which hir fader hadde
With hire al priveli sche ladde,
And with Jason at time set
Awey sche stal and fond no let,   3900
And straght sche goth hire unto schipe
Of Grece with that felaschipe,
And thei anon drowe up the seil.
And al that nyht this was conseil,
Bot erly, whan the sonne schon,
Men syhe hou that thei were agon,
And come unto the king and tolde:
And he the sothe knowe wolde,
And axeth where his dowhter was.
Ther was no word bot 'Out, Allas!'   3910
Sche was ago. The moder wepte,
The fader as a wod man lepte,
And gan the time forto warie,
And swor his oth he wol noght tarie,
That with caliphe and with galeie
The same cours, the same weie,
Which Jason tok, he wolde take,
If that he mihte him overtake.
To this thei seiden alle yee:
Anon thei weren ate see,   3920
And alle, as who seith, at a word
Thei gon withinne schipes bord,
The sail goth up, and forth thei strauhte.
Bot non espleit therof thei cauhte,
And so thei tornen hom ayein,
For al that labour was in vein.
  Jason to Grece with his preie
Goth thurgh the see the rihte weie:
Whan he ther com and men it tolde,
Thei maden joie yonge and olde.   3930
Eson, whan that he wiste of this,
Hou that his sone comen is,
And hath achieved that he soughte
And hom with him Medea broughte,

73

In al the wyde world was non
So glad a man as he was on.
Togedre ben these lovers tho,
Til that thei hadden sones tuo,
Wherof thei weren bothe glade,
And olde Eson gret joie made   3940
To sen th'encress of his lignage;
For he was of so gret an age,
That men awaiten every day,
Whan that he scholde gon away.
Jason, which sih his fader old,
Upon Medea made him bold,
Of art magique, which sche couthe,
And preith hire that his fader youthe
Sche wolde make ayeinward newe:
And sche, that was toward him trewe,   3950
Behihte him that sche wolde it do,
Whan that sche time sawh therto.
Bot what sche dede in that matiere
It is a wonder thing to hiere,
Bot yit for the novellerie
I thenke tellen a partie.

   Thus it befell upon a nyht,
Whan ther was noght bot sterreliht,
Sche was vanyssht riht as hir liste,
That no wyht bot hirself it wiste,   3960
And that was ate mydnyht tyde.
The world was stille on every side;
With open hed and fot al bare,
Hir her tosprad, sche gan to fare,
Upon hir clothes gert sche was,
Al specheles and on the gras
Sche glod forth as an addre doth:
Non otherwise sche ne goth,
Til sche cam to the freisshe flod,
And there a while sche withstod.   3970
Thries sche torned hire aboute,
And thries ek sche gan doun loute

And in the flod sche wette hir her,
And thries on the water ther
Sche gaspeth with a drecchinge onde,
And tho sche tok hir speche on honde.
Ferst sche began to clepe and calle
Upward unto the sterres alle,
To wynd, to air, to see, to lond
Sche preide, and ek hield up hir hond,   3980
To Echates and gan to crie,
Which is goddesse of sorcerie.
Sche seide, 'Helpeth at this nede,
And as ye maden me to spede,
Whan Jason cam the flees to seche,
So help me nou, I you beseche.'
With that sche loketh and was war,
Doun fro the sky ther cam a char,
The which dragouns aboute drowe:
And tho sche gan hir hed doun bowe,   3990
And up sche styh, and faire and wel
Sche drof forth bothe char and whel
Above in th'air among the skyes.
The lond of Crete and tho parties
Sche soughte, and faste gan hire hye,
And there upon the hulles hyhe
Of Othrin and Olimpe also,
And ek of othre hulles mo,
Sche fond and gadreth herbes suote,
Sche pulleth up som be the rote,   4000
And manye with a knyf sche scherth,
And alle into hir char sche berth.
Thus whan sche hath the hulles sought,
The flodes ther foryat sche nought,
Eridian and Amphrisos,
Peneie and ek Spercheïdos,
To hem sche wente and ther sche nom
Bothe of the water and the fom,
The sond and ek the smale stones,
Whiche as sche ches out for the nones,   4010

And of the Rede See a part,
That was behovelich to hire art,
Sche tok, and after that aboute
Sche soughte sondri sedes oute
In feldes and in many greves,
And ek a part sche tok of leves:
Bot thing which mihte hire most availe
Sche fond in Crete and in Thessaile.

    In daies and in nyhtes nyne,
With gret travaile and with gret pyne,   4020
Sche was pourveid of every piece,
And torneth homward into Grece.
Before the gates of Eson
Hir char sche let awai to gon,
And tok out ferst that was therinne;
For tho sche thoghte to beginne
Such thing as semeth impossible,
And made hirselven invisible,
As sche that was with air enclosed
And mihte of noman be desclosed.   4030
Sche tok up turves of the lond
Withoute helpe of mannes hond,
Al heled with the grene gras,
Of which an alter mad ther was
Unto Echates the goddesse
Of art magique and the maistresse,
And eft an other to Juvente,
As sche which dede hir hole entente.
Tho tok sche fieldwode and verveyne,
Of herbes ben noght betre tueine,   4040
Of which anon withoute let
These alters ben aboute set:
Tuo sondri puttes faste by
Sche made, and with that hastely
A wether which was blak sche slouh,
And out therof the blod sche drouh
And dede into the pettes tuo;
Warm melk sche putte also therto

With hony meynd: and in such wise
Sche gan to make hir sacrifice,   4050
And cride and preide forth withal
To Pluto the god infernal,
And to the queene Proserpine.
And so sche soghte out al the line
Of hem that longen to that craft,
Behinde was no name laft,
And preide hem alle, as sche wel couthe,
To grante Eson his ferste youthe.
    This olde Eson broght forth was tho,
Awei sche bad alle othre go   4060
Upon peril that mihte falle;
And with that word thei wenten alle,
And leften there hem tuo al one.
And tho sche gan to gaspe and gone,
And made signes manyon,
And seide hir wordes therupon;
So that with spellinge of hir charmes
Sche tok Eson in bothe hire armes,
And made him forto slepe faste,
And him upon hire herbes caste.   4070
The blake wether tho sche tok,
And hiewh the fleissh, as doth a cok;
On either alter part sche leide,
And with the charmes that sche seide
A fyr doun fro the sky alyhte
And made it forto brenne lyhte.
Bot whan Medea sawh it brenne,
Anon sche gan to sterte and renne
The fyri aulters al aboute:
Ther was no beste which goth oute   4080
More wylde than sche semeth ther:
Aboute hir schuldres hyng hir her,
As thogh sche were oute of hir mynde
And torned in an other kynde.
Tho lay ther certein wode cleft,
Of which the pieces nou and eft

Sche made hem in the pettes wete,
And put hem in the fyri hete,
And tok the brond with al the blase,
And thries sche began to rase   4090
Aboute Eson, ther as he slepte;
And eft with water, which sche kepte,
Sche made a cercle aboute him thries,
And eft with fyr of sulphre twyes:
Ful many an other thing sche dede,
Which is noght writen in this stede.
Bot tho sche ran so up and doun,
Sche made many a wonder soun,
Somtime lich unto the cock,
Somtime unto the laverock,   4100
Somtime kacleth as a hen,
Somtime spekth as don the men:
And riht so as hir jargoun strangeth,
In sondri wise hir forme changeth,
Sche semeth faie and no womman;
For with the craftes that sche can
Sche was, as who seith, a goddesse,
And what hir liste, more or lesse,
Sche dede, in bokes as we finde,
That passeth over manneskinde.   4110
Bot who that wole of wondres hiere,
What thing sche wroghte in this matiere,
To make an ende of that sche gan,
Such merveile herde nevere man.

   Apointed in the newe mone,
Whan it was time forto done,
Sche sette a caldron on the fyr,
In which was al the hole atir,
Wheron the medicine stod,
Of jus, of water and of blod,   4120
And let it buile in such a plit,
Til that sche sawh the spume whyt;
And tho sche caste in rynde and rote,
And sed and flour that was for bote,

With many an herbe and many a ston,
Wherof sche hath ther many on:
And ek Cimpheius the serpent
To hire hath alle his scales lent,
Chelidre hire yaf his addres skin,
And sche to builen caste hem in;   4130
A part ek of the horned oule,
The which men hiere on nyhtes houle;
And of a raven, which was told
Of nyne hundred wynter old,
Sche tok the hed with al the bile;
And as the medicine it wile,
Sche tok therafter the bouele
Of the seewolf, and for the hele
Of Eson, with a thousand mo
Of thinges that sche hadde tho,   4140
In that caldroun togedre as blyve
Sche putte, and tok thanne of olyve
A drie branche hem with to stere,
The which anon gan floure and bere
And waxe al freissh and grene ayein.
Whan sche this vertu hadde sein,
Sche let the leste drope of alle
Upon the bare flor doun falle;
Anon ther sprong up flour and gras,
Where as the drope falle was,   4150
And wox anon al medwe-grene,
So that it mihte wel be sene.
Medea thanne knew and wiste
Hir medicine is forto triste,
And goth to Eson ther he lay,
And tok a swerd was of assay,
With which a wounde upon his side
Sche made, that therout mai slyde
The blod withinne, which was old
And sek and trouble and fieble and cold.   4160
And tho sche tok unto his us
Of herbes al the beste jus,

79

And poured it into his wounde;
That made his veynes fulle and sounde:
And tho sche made his wounde clos,
And tok his hand, and up he ros;
And tho sche yaf him drinke a drauhte,
Of which his youthe ayein he cauhte,
His hed, his herte and his visage
Lich unto twenty wynter age;   4170
Hise hore heres were away,
And lich unto the freisshe Maii,
Whan passed ben the colde schoures,
Riht so recovereth he his floures.

VII

The Tale of Tereus and Procne (v. 5551–6047)

THER was a real noble king,
And riche of alle worldes thing,
Which of his propre enheritance
Athenes hadde in governance,
And who so thenke therupon,
His name was king Pandion.
Tuo douhtres hadde he be his wif,
The whiche he lovede as his lif;
The ferste douhter Progne hihte,
And the secounde, as sche wel mihte,   5560
Was cleped faire Philomene,
To whom fell after mochel tene.
The fader of his pourveance
His doughter Progne wolde avance,
And yaf hire unto mariage
A worthi king of hih lignage,
A noble kniht eke of his hond,
So was he kid in every lond,
Of Trace he hihte Tereüs;
The clerk Ovide telleth thus.   5570

This Tereüs his wif hom ladde,
A lusti lif with hire he hadde;
Til it befell upon a tyde,
This Progne, as sche lay him besyde,
Bethoughte hir hou it mihte be
That sche hir soster myhte se,
And to hir lord hir will sche seide,
With goodly wordes and him preide
That sche to hire mihte go:
And if it liked him noght so,   5580
That thanne he wolde himselve wende,
Or elles be som other sende,
Which mihte hire diere soster griete,
And schape hou that thei mihten miete.
Hir lord anon to that he herde
Yaf his acord, and thus ansuerde:
'I wole,' he seide, 'for thi sake
The weie after thi soster take
Miself, and bringe hire, if I may.'
And sche with that, there as he lay,   5590
Began him in hire armes clippe,
And kist him with hir softe lippe,
And seide, 'Sire, grant mercy.'
And he sone after was redy,
And tok his leve forto go;
In sori time dede he so.
    This Tereüs goth forth to schipe
With him and with his felaschipe;
Be see the rihte cours he nam,
Into the contre til he cam,   5600
Wher Philomene was duellinge,
And of hir soster the tidinge
He tolde, and tho thei weren glade,
And mochel joie of him thei made.
The fader and the moder bothe
To leve here douhter weren lothe,
Bot if thei weren in presence;
And natheles at reverence

Of him, that wolde himself travaile,
Thei wolden noght he scholde faile   5610
Of that he preide, and yive hire leve:
And sche, that wolde noght beleve,
In alle haste made hire yare
Toward hir soster forto fare,
With Tereüs and forth sche wente.
And he with al his hole entente,
Whan sche was fro hir frendes go,
Assoteth of hire love so,
His yhe myhte he noght withholde,
That he ne moste on hir beholde;   5620
And with the sihte he gan desire,
And sette his oghne herte on fyre;
And fyr, whan it to tow aprocheth,
To him anon the strengthe acrocheth,
Til with his hete it be devoured,
The tow ne mai noght be socoured.
And so that tirant raviner,
Whan that sche was in his pouer,
And he therto sawh time and place,
As he that lost hath alle grace,   5630
Foryat he was a wedded man,
And in a rage on hire he ran,
Riht as a wolf which takth his preie.
And sche began to crie and preie,
'O fader, o mi moder diere,
Nou help!' Bot thei ne mihte it hiere,
And sche was of to litel myht
Defense ayein so ruide a knyht
To make, whanne he was so wod
That he no reson understod,   5640
Bot hield hire under in such wise,
That sche ne myhte noght arise,
Bot lay oppressed and desesed,
As if a goshauk hadde sesed
A brid, which dorste noght for fere
Remue: and thus this tirant there

Beraft hire such thing as men sein
Mai neveremor be yolde ayein,
And that was the virginite:
Of such ravine it was pite.   5650
   Bot whan sche to hirselven com,
And of hir meschief hiede nom,
And knew hou that sche was no maide,
With wofull herte thus sche saide:
'O thou of alle men the worste,
Wher was ther evere man that dorste
Do such a dede as thou hast do?
That dai schal falle, I hope so,
That I schal telle out al mi fille,
And with mi speche I schal fulfille   5660
The wyde world in brede and lengthe.
That thou hast do to me be strengthe,
If I among the poeple duelle,
Unto the poeple I schal it telle;
And if I be withinne wall
Of stones closed, thanne I schal
Unto the stones clepe and crie,
And tellen hem thi felonie;
And if I to the wodes wende,
Ther schal I tellen tale and ende,   5670
And crie it to the briddes oute,
That thei schul hiere it al aboute.
For I so loude it schal reherce,
That my vois schal the hevene perce,
That it schal soune in goddes ere.
Ha, false man, where is thi fere?
O mor cruel than eny beste,
Hou hast thou holden thi beheste
Which thou unto my soster madest?
O thou, which alle love ungladest,   5680
And art ensample of alle untrewe,
Nou wolde god mi soster knewe,
Of thin untrouthe, hou that it stod!'
And he than as a lyon wod

With hise unhappi handes stronge
Hire cauhte be the tresses longe,
With whiche he bond ther bothe hire armes,
That was a fieble dede of armes,
And to the grounde anon hire caste,
And out he clippeth also faste   5690
Hire tunge with a peire scheres.
So what with blod and what with teres
Out of hire yhe and of hir mouth,
He made hire faire face uncouth:
Sche lay swounende unto the deth,
Ther was unethes eny breth;
Bot yit whan he hire tunge refte,
A litel part therof belefte,
Bot sche with al no word mai soune,
Bot chitre and as a brid jargoune.   5700
And natheles that wode hound
Hir bodi hent up fro the ground,
And sente hir there as be his wille
Sche scholde abyde in prison stille
For everemo: bot nou tak hiede
What after fell of this misdede.
    Whanne al this meschief was befalle,
This Tereüs, that foule him falle,
Unto his contre hom he tyh;
And whan he com his paleis nyh,   5710
His wif al redi there him kepte.
Whan he hir sih, anon he wepte,
And that he dede for deceite,
For sche began to axe him streite,
'Wher is mi soster?' And he seide
That sche was ded; and Progne abreide,
As sche that was a wofull wif,
And stod betuen hire deth and lif,
Of that sche herde such tidinge:
Bot for sche sih hire lord wepinge,   5720
She wende noght bot alle trouthe,
And hadde wel the more routhe.

The perles weren tho forsake,
To hire and blake clothes take;
As sche that was gentil and kinde,
In worschipe of hir sostres mynde
Sche made a riche enterement,
For sche fond non amendement
To syghen or to sobbe more:
So was ther guile under the gore.   5730
   Nou leve we this king and queene,
And torne ayein to Philomene,
As I began to tellen erst.
Whan sche cam into prison ferst,
It thoghte a kinges douhter strange
To maken so soudein a change
Fro welthe unto so grete a wo;
And sche began to thenke tho,
Thogh sche be mouthe nothing preide,
Withinne hir herte thus sche seide: 5740
'O thou, almyhty Jupiter,
That hihe sist and lokest fer,
Thou soffrest many a wrong-doinge,
And yit it is noght thi willinge.
To thee ther mai nothing ben hid,
Thou wost hou it is me betid:
I wolde I hadde noght be bore,
For thanne I hadde noght forlore
Mi speche and mi virginite.
Bot, goode lord, al is in thee,   5750
Whan thou therof wolt do vengance
And schape mi deliverance.'
And evere among this ladi wepte,
And thoghte that sche nevere kepte
To ben a worldes womman more,
And that sche wissheth everemore.
Bot ofte unto hir soster diere
Hire herte spekth in this manere,
And seide, 'Ha, soster, if ye knewe
Of myn astat, ye wolde rewe,   5760

I trowe, and my deliverance
Ye wolde schape, and do vengance
On him that is so fals a man:
And natheles, so as I can,
I wol you sende som tokninge,
Wherof ye schul have knowlechinge
Of thing I wot, that schal you lothe,
The which you toucheth and me bothe.'
And tho withinne a whyle als tyt
Sche waf a cloth of selk al whyt   5770
With lettres and ymagerie,
In which was al the felonie,
Which Tereüs to hire hath do;
And lappede it togedre tho
And sette hir signet therupon
And sende it unto Progne anon.
The messager which forth it bar,
What it amonteth is noght war;
And natheles to Progne he goth
And prively takth hire the cloth,   5780
And wente ayein riht as he cam,
The court of him non hiede nam.

   Whan Progne of Philomene herde,
Sche wolde knowe hou that it ferde,
And opneth that the man hath broght,
And wot therby what hath be wroght
And what meschief ther is befalle.
In swoune tho sche gan doun falle,
And efte aros and gan to stonde,
And eft sche takth the cloth on honde,   5790
Behield the lettres and th'ymages;
Bot ate laste, 'Of suche oultrages,'
Sche seith, 'wepinge is noght the bote:'
And swerth, if that sche live mote,
It schal be venged otherwise.
And with that sche gan hire avise
Hou ferst sche mihte unto hire winne
Hir soster, that noman withinne,

Bot only thei that were suore,
It scholde knowe, and schop therfore 5800
That Tereüs nothing it wiste;
And yit riht as hirselven liste,
Hir soster was delivered sone
Out of prison, and be the mone
To Progne sche was broght be nyhte.
  Whan ech of other hadde a sihte,
In chambre, ther thei were al one,
Thei maden many a pitous mone;
Bot Progne most of sorwe made,
Which sihe hir soster pale and fade 5810
And specheles and deshonoured,
Of that sche hadde be defloured;
And ek upon hir lord sche thoghte,
Of that he so untreuly wroghte
And hadde his espousaile broke.
Sche makth a vou it schal be wroke,
And with that word sche kneleth doun
Wepinge in gret devocioun:
Unto Cupide and to Venus
Sche preide, and seide thanne thus: 5820
'O ye, to whom nothing asterte
Of love mai, for every herte
Ye knowe, as ye that ben above
The god and the goddesse of love;
Ye witen wel that evere yit
With al mi will and al my wit,
Sith ferst ye schopen me to wedde,
That I lay with mi lord abedde,
I have be trewe in mi degre,
And evere thoghte forto be, 5830
And nevere love in other place,
Bot al only the king of Trace,
Which is mi lord and I his wif.
Bot nou allas this wofull strif!
That I him thus ayeinward finde
The most untrewe and most unkinde

87

That evere in ladi armes lay.
And wel I wot that he ne may
Amende his wrong, it is so gret;
For he to lytel of me let,   5840
Whan he myn oughne soster tok,
And me that am his wif forsok.'
    Lo, thus to Venus and Cupide
Sche preide, and furthermor sche cride
Unto Appollo the hiheste,
And seide, 'O myghti god of reste,
Thou do vengance of this debat.
Mi soster and al hire astat
Thou wost, and hou sche hath forlore
Hir maidenhod, and I therfore   5850
In al the world schal bere a blame
Of that mi soster hath a schame,
That Tereüs to hire I sente:
And wel thou wost that myn entente
Was al for worschipe and for goode.
O lord, that yifst the lives fode
To every wyht, I prei thee hiere
Thes wofull sostres that ben hiere,
And let ous noght to the ben lothe;
We ben thin oghne wommen bothe.'   5860
    Thus pleigneth Progne and axeth wreche,
And thogh hire soster lacke speche,
To him that alle thinges wot
Hire sorwe is noght the lasse hot:
Bot he that thanne had herd hem tuo,
Him oughte have sorwed everemo
For sorwe which was hem betuene.
With signes pleigneth Philomene,
And Progne seith, 'It schal be wreke,
That al the world therof schal speke.'   5870
And Progne tho seknesse feigneth,
Wherof unto hir lord sche pleigneth,
And preith sche moste hire chambres kepe,
And as hir liketh wake and slepe.

And he hire granteth to be so;
And thus togedre ben thei tuo,
That wolde him bot a litel good.
Nou herk hierafter hou it stod
Of wofull auntres that befelle:
Thes sostres, that ben bothe felle,—   5880
And that was noght on hem along,
Bot onliche on the grete wrong
Which Tereüs hem hadde do,—
Thei schopen forto venge hem tho.
　This Tereüs be Progne his wif
A sone hath, which as his lif
He loveth, and Ithis he hihte:
His moder wiste wel sche mihte
Do Tereüs no more grief
Than sle this child, which was so lief.   5890
Thus sche, that was, as who seith, mad
Of wo, which hath hir overlad,
Withoute insihte of moderhede
Foryat pite and loste drede,
And in hir chambre prively
This child withouten noise or cry
Sche slou, and hieu him al to pieces:
And after with diverse spieces
The fleissh, whan it was so toheewe,
Sche takth, and makth therof a sewe,   5900
With which the fader at his mete
Was served, til he hadde him ete;
That he ne wiste hou that it stod,
Bot thus his oughne fleissh and blod
Himself devoureth ayein kinde,
As he that was tofore unkinde.
And thanne, er that he were arise,
For that he scholde ben agrise,
To schewen him the child was ded,
This Philomene tok the hed   5910
Betwen tuo disshes, and al wrothe
Tho comen forth the sostres bothe,

89

And setten it upon the bord.
And Progne tho began the word,
And seide, 'O werste of alle wicke,
Of conscience whom no pricke
Mai stere, lo, what thou hast do!
Lo, hier ben nou we sostres tuo;
O raviner, lo hier thi preie,
With whom so falsliche on the weie   5920
Thou hast thi tirannye wroght.
Lo, nou it is somdel aboght,
And bet it schal, for of thi dede
The world schal evere singe and rede
In remembrance of thi defame:
For thou to love hast do such schame,
That it schal nevere be foryete.'
With that he sterte up fro the mete,
And schof the bord unto the flor,
And cauhte a swerd anon and suor   5930
That thei scholde of his handes dye.
And thei unto the goddes crie
Begunne with so loude a stevene,
That thei were herd unto the hevene;
And in a twinclinge of an yhe
The goddes, that the meschief syhe,
Here formes changen alle thre.
Echon of hem in his degre
Was torned into briddes kinde;
Diverseliche, as men mai finde,   5940
After th'astat that thei were inne,
Here formes were set atwinne.
And as it telleth in the tale,
The ferst into a nyhtingale
Was schape, and that was Philomene,
Which in the wynter is noght sene,
For thanne ben the leves falle
And naked ben the buisshes alle.
For after that sche was a brid,
Hir will was evere to ben hid,   5950

And forto duelle in prive place,
That noman scholde sen hir face
For schame, which mai noght be lassed,
Of thing that was tofore passed,
Whan that sche loste hir maidenhiede:
For evere upon hir wommanhiede,
Thogh that the goddes wolde hire change,
Sche thenkth, and is the more strange,
And halt hir clos the wyntres day.
Bot whan the wynter goth away, 5960
And that Nature the goddesse
Wole of hir oughne fre largesse
With herbes and with floures bothe
The feldes and the medwes clothe,
And ek the wodes and the greves
Ben heled al with grene leves,
So that a brid hire hyde mai,
Betwen Averil and March and Maii,
Sche that the wynter hield hir clos,
For pure schame and noght aros, 5970
Whan that sche seth the bowes thikke,
And that ther is no bare sticke,
Bot al is hid with leves grene,
To wode comth this Philomene
And makth hir ferste yeres flyht;
Wher as sche singeth day and nyht,
And in hir song al openly
Sche makth hir pleignte and seith, 'O why,
O why ne were I yit a maide?'
For so these olde wise saide, 5980
Which understoden what sche mente,
Hire notes ben of such entente.
And ek thei seide hou in hir song
Sche makth gret joie and merthe among,
And seith, 'Ha, nou I am a brid,
Ha, nou mi face mai ben hid:
Thogh I have lost mi maidenhede,
Schal noman se my chekes rede.'

Thus medleth sche with joie wo
And with hir sorwe merthe also,   5990
So that of loves maladie
Sche makth diverse melodie,
And seith love is a wofull blisse,
A wisdom which can noman wisse,
A lusti fievere, a wounde softe:
This note sche reherceth ofte
To hem whiche understonde hir tale.
Nou have I of this nyhtingale,
Which erst was cleped Philomene,
Told al that evere I wolde mene,   6000
Bothe of hir forme and of hir note,
Wherof men mai the storie note.

   And of hir soster Progne I finde,
Hou sche was torned out of kinde
Into a swalwe swift of winge,
Which ek in wynter lith swounynge,
Ther as sche mai nothing be sene:
Bot whan the world is woxe grene
And comen is the somertide,
Than fleth sche forth and ginth to chide,   6010
And chitreth out in hir langage
What falshod is in mariage,
And telleth in a maner speche
Of Tereüs the spousebreche.
Sche wol noght in the wodes duelle,
For sche wolde openliche telle;
And ek for that sche was a spouse,
Among the folk sche comth to house,
To do thes wyves understonde
The falshod of hire housebonde,   6020
That thei of hem be war also,
For ther ben manye untrewe of tho.
Thus ben the sostres briddes bothe,
And ben toward the men so lothe,
That thei ne wole of pure schame
Unto no mannes hand be tame;

For evere it duelleth in here mynde
Of that thei founde a man unkinde,
And that was false Tereüs.
If such on be amonges ous   6030
I not, bot his condicion
Men sein in every region
Withinne toune and ek withoute
Nou regneth comunliche aboute.
And natheles in remembrance
I wol declare what vengance
The goddes hadden him ordeined,
Of that the sostres hadden pleigned:
For anon after he was changed
And from his oghne kinde stranged,   6040
A lappewincke mad he was,
And thus he hoppeth on the gras,
And on his hed ther stant upriht
A creste in tokne he was a kniht;
And yit unto this dai men seith,
A lappewincke hath lore his feith
And is the brid falseste of alle.

VIII

*The confessor's final counsel. The lover's prayer to Venus
and dream of Cupid's company; his healing and absolution and
farewell to love (viii. 2013–end)*

Confessor   FORTUNE, thogh sche be noght stable,
Yit at som time is favorable
To hem that ben of love trewe.
Bot certes it is forto rewe
To se love ayein kinde falle,
For that makth sore a man to falle,
As thou myht of tofore rede.
Forthi, my sone, I wolde rede   2020

To lete al other love aweie,
Bot if it be thurgh such a weie
As love and reson wolde acorde.
For elles, if that thou descorde,
And take lust as doth a beste,
Thi love mai noght ben honeste;
For be no skile that I finde
Such lust is noght of loves kinde.

Mi fader, hou so that it stonde,
Youre tale is herd and understonde,   2030
As thing which worthi is to hiere,
Of gret ensample and gret matiere,
Wherof, my fader, god you quyte.
Bot in this point miself aquite
I mai riht wel, that nevere yit
I was assoted in my wit,
Bot only in that worthi place
Wher alle lust and alle grace
Is set, if that danger ne were.
Bot that is al my moste fere: 2040
I not what ye fortune acompte,
Bot what thing danger mai amonte
I wot wel, for I have assaied;
For whan myn herte is best arraied
And I have al my wit thurghsoght
Of love to beseche hire oght,
For al that evere I skile may,
I am concluded with a nay:
That o sillable hath overthrowe
A thousend wordes on a rowe   2050
Of suche as I best speke can;
Thus am I bot a lewed man.
Bot, fader, for ye ben a clerk
Of love, and this matiere is derk,
And I can evere leng the lasse,
Bot yit I mai noght let it passe,
Youre hole conseil I beseche,
That ye me be som weie teche

What is my beste, as for an ende.

Mi sone, unto the trouthe wende   2060
Now wol I for the love of thee,
And lete alle othre truffles be.
   The more that the nede is hyh,
The more it nedeth to be slyh
To him which hath the nede on honde.
I have wel herd and understonde,
Mi sone, al that thou hast me seid,
And ek of that thou hast me preid,
Nou at this time that I schal
As for conclusioun final   2070
Conseile upon thi nede sette:
So thenke I finaly to knette
This cause, where it is tobroke,
And make an ende of that is spoke.
For I behihte thee that yifte
Ferst whan thou come under my schrifte,
That thogh I toward Venus were,
Yit spak I suche wordes there,
That for the presthod which I have,
Min ordre and min astat to save,   2080
I seide I wolde of myn office
To vertu more than to vice
Encline, and teche thee mi lore.
Forthi to speken overmore
Of love, which thee mai availe,
Tak love where it mai noght faile:
For as of this which thou art inne,
Be that thou seist it is a sinne,
And sinne mai no pris deserve,
Withoute pris and who schal serve,   2090
I not what profit myhte availe.
Thus folweth it, if thou travaile
Wher thou no profit hast ne pris,
Thou art toward thiself unwis:
And sett thou myhtest lust atteigne,
Of every lust th'ende is a peine,

And every peine is good to fle;
So it is wonder thing to se,
Why such a thing schal be desired.
The more that a stock is fyred, 2100
The rathere into aisshe it torneth;
The fot which in the weie sporneth
Fulofte his heved hath overthrowe;
Thus love is blind and can noght knowe
Wher that he goth, til he be falle:
Forthi, bot if it so befalle
With good conseil that he be lad,
Him oghte forto ben adrad.
For conseil passeth alle thing
To him which thenkth to ben a king; 2110
And every man for his partie
A kingdom hath to justefie,
That is to sein his oghne dom.
If he misreule that kingdom,
He lest himself, and that is more
Than if he loste schip and ore
And al the worldes good withal:
For what man that in special
Hath noght himself, he hath noght elles,
Nomor the perles than the schelles; 2120
Al is to him of o value:
Thogh he hadde at his retenue
The wyde world riht as he wolde,
Whan he his herte hath noght withholde
Toward himself, al is in vein.
And thus, my sone, I wolde sein,
As I seide er, that thou aryse,
Er that thou falle in such a wise
That thou ne myht thiself rekevere;
For love, which that blind was evere, 2130
Makth alle his servantz blinde also.
My sone, and if thou have be so,
Yit is it time to withdrawe,
And set thin herte under that lawe,

The which of reson is governed
And noght of will. And to be lerned,
Ensamples thou hast many on
Of now and ek of time gon,
That every lust is bot a while;
And who that wole himself beguile,   2140
He may the rathere be deceived.
Mi Sone, now thou hast conceived
Somwhat of that I wolde mene;
Hierafterward it schal be sene
If that thou lieve upon mi lore;
For I can do to thee nomore
Bot teche thee the rihte weie:
Now ches if thou wolt live or deie.

Amans   Mi fader, so as I have herd
Your tale, bot it were ansuerd,   2150
I were mochel forto blame.
Mi wo to you is bot a game,
That fielen noght of that I fiele;
The fielinge of a mannes hiele
Mai noght be likned to the herte:
I mai noght, thogh I wolde, asterte,
And ye be fre from al the peine
Of love, wherof I me pleigne.
It is riht esi to comaunde;
The hert which fre goth on the launde   2160
Not of an oxe what him eileth;
It falleth ofte a man merveileth
Of that he seth an other fare,
Bot if he knewe himself the fare,
And felt it as it is in soth,
He scholde don riht as he doth,
Or elles werse in his degre:
For wel I wot, and so do ye,
That love hath evere yit ben used,
So mot I nedes ben excused.   2170
Bot, fader, if ye wolde thus

Unto Cupide and to Venus
Be frendlich toward mi querele,
So that myn herte were in hele
Of love which is in mi briest,
I wot wel thanne a betre prest
Was nevere mad to my behove.
Bot al the whiles that I hove
In noncertein betwen the tuo,
And not if I to wel or wo   2180
Schal torne, that is al my drede,
So that I not what is to rede.
Bot for final conclusion
I thenke a supplicacion
With pleine wordes and expresse
Wryte unto Venus the goddesse,
The which I preie you to bere
And bringe ayein a good ansuere.

Tho was betwen mi prest and me
Debat and gret perplexete: 2190
Mi resoun understod him wel,
And knew it was soth everydel
That he hath seid, bot noght forthi
Mi will hath nothing set therby.
For techinge of so wis a port
Is unto love of no desport;
Yit myhte nevere man beholde
Reson, wher love was withholde;
Thei be noght of o governance.
And thus we fellen in distance,   2200
Mi prest and I, bot I spak faire,
And thurgh mi wordes debonaire
Thanne ate laste we acorden,
So that he seith he wol recorden
To speke and stonde upon mi syde
To Venus bothe and to Cupide;
And bad me wryte what I wolde,
And seith me trewly that he scholde

Mi lettre bere unto the queene.
And I sat doun upon the grene   2210
Fulfilt of loves fantasie,
And with the teres of myn ÿe
In stede of enke I gan to wryte
The wordes whiche I wolde endite
Unto Cupide and to Venus,
And in mi lettre I seide thus:

    THE wofull peine of loves maladie,
Ayein the which mai no phisique availe,
Min herte hath so bewhaped with sotie,
That wher so that I reste or I travaile,   2220
I finde it evere redy to assaile
Mi resoun, which that can him noght defende:
Thus seche I help, wherof I mihte amende.

Ferst to Nature if that I me compleigne,
Ther finde I hou that every creature
Som time ayer hath love in his demeine,
So that the litel wrenne in his mesure
Hath yit of kinde a love under his cure;
And I bot on desire, of which I misse:
And thus, bot I, hath every kinde his blisse.   2230

The resoun of my wit it overpasseth,
Of that Nature techeth me the weie
To love, and yit no certein sche compasseth
Hou I schal spede, and thus betwen the tweie
I stonde, and not if I schal live or deie.
For thogh reson ayein my will debate,
I mai noght fle, that I ne love algate.

Upon miself is thilke tale come,
Hou whilom Pan, which is the god of kinde,
With love wrastlede and was overcome: 2240
For evere I wrastle and evere I am behinde,
That I no strengthe in al min herte finde,

99

Wherof that I mai stonden eny throwe;
So fer mi wit with love is overthrowe.

Whom nedeth help, he mot his helpe crave,
Or helpeles he schal his nede spille:
Pleinly thurghsoght my wittes alle I have,
Bot non of hem can helpe after mi wille;
And als so wel I mihte sitte stille,
As preie unto mi lady eny helpe: 2250
Thus wot I noght wherof miself to helpe.

Unto the grete Jove and if I bidde,
To do me grace of thilke swete tunne,
Which under keie in his celier amidde
Lith couched, that fortune is overrunne,
Bot of the bitter cuppe I have begunne,
I not hou ofte, and thus finde I no game;
For evere I axe and evere it is the same.

I se the world stonde evere upon eschange,
Nou wyndes loude, and nou the weder softe;   2260
I mai sen ek the grete mone change,
And thing which nou is lowe is eft alofte;
The dredfull werres into pes fulofte
Thei torne; and evere is Danger in o place,
Which wol noght change his will to do me grace.

Bot upon this the grete clerc Ovide,
Of love whan he makth his remembrance,
He seith ther is the blinde god Cupide,
The which hath love under his governance,
And in his hond with many a fyri lance   2270
He woundeth ofte, ther he wol noght hele;
And that somdiel is cause of mi querele.

Ovide ek seith that love to parforne
Stant in the hond of Venus the goddesse,
Bot whan sche takth hir conseil with Satorne,

Ther is no grace, and in that time, I gesse,
Began mi love, of which myn hevynesse
Is now and evere schal, bot if I spede:
So wot I noght miself what is to rede.

Forthi to you, Cupide and Venus bothe,   2280
With al myn hertes obeissance I preie,
If ye were ate ferste time wrothe,
Whan I began to love, as I you seie,
Nou stynt, and do thilke infortune aweie,
So that Danger, which stant of retenue
With my ladi, his place mai remue.

O thou Cupide, god of loves lawe,
That with thi dart brennende hast set afyre
Min herte, do that wounde be withdrawe,
Or yif me salve such as I desire: 2290
For service in thi court withouten hyre
To me, which evere yit have kept thin heste,
Mai nevere be to loves lawe honeste.

O thou, gentile Venus, loves queene,
Withoute gult thou dost on me thi wreche;
Thou wost my peine is evere aliche grene
For love, and yit I mai it noght areche:
This wold I for my laste word beseche,
That thou mi love aquite as I deserve,
Or elles do me pleinly forto sterve.   2300

    Whanne I this supplicacioun
With good deliberacioun,
In such a wise as ye nou wite,
Hadde after min entente write
Unto Cupide and to Venus,
This prest, which hihte Genius,
It tok on honde to presente,
On my message and forth he wente
To Venus, forto wite hire wille.

And I bod in the place stille, 2310
And was there bot a litel while,
Noght full the montance of a mile,
Whan I behield and sodeinly
I sih wher Venus stod me by.
So as I myhte, under a tre
To grounde I fell upon mi kne,
And preide hire forto do me grace:
Sche caste hire chiere upon mi face,
And as it were halvinge a game
Sche axeth me what is mi name. 2320
'Ma dame,' I seide, 'John Gower.'
'Now John,' quod sche, 'in my pouer
Thou most as of thi love stonde;
For I thi bille have understonde,
In which to Cupide and to me
Somdiel thou hast compleigned thee,
And somdiel to Nature also.
Bot that schal stonde among you tuo,
For therof have I noght to done;
For Nature is under the mone 2330
Maistresse of every lives kinde,
Bot if so be that sche mai finde
Som holy man that wol withdrawe
His kindly lust ayein hir lawe;
Bot sielde whanne it falleth so,
For fewe men ther ben of tho,
Bot of these othre ynowe be,
Whiche of here oghne nycete
Ayein Nature and hire office
Deliten hem in sondri vice, 2340
Wherof that sche fulofte hath pleigned,
And ek my court it hath desdeigned
And evere schal; for it receiveth
Non such that kinde so deceiveth.
For al onliche of gentil love
Mi court stant alle courtz above
And takth noght into retenue

Bot thing which is to kinde due,
For elles it schal be refused.
Wherof I holde thee excused,   2350
For it is manye daies gon,
That thou amonges hem were on
Which of my court hast ben withholde;
So that the more I am beholde
Of thi desese to commune,
And to remue that fortune,
Which manye daies hath the grieved.
Bot if my conseil mai be lieved,
Thou schalt ben esed er thou go
Of thilke unsely jolif wo,   2360
Wherof thou seist thin herte is fyred:
Bot as of that thou hast desired
After the sentence of thi bille,
Thou most therof don at my wille,
And I therof me wole avise.
For be thou hol, it schal suffise:
Mi medicine is noght to sieke
For thee and for suche olde sieke,
Noght al per chance as ye it wolden,
Bot so as ye be reson scholden,   2370
Acordant unto loves kinde.
For in the plit which I thee finde,
So as mi court it hath awarded,
Thou schalt be duely rewarded;
And if thou woldest more crave,
It is no riht that thou it have.'

   Venus, which stant withoute lawe
In noncertein, bot as men drawe
Of rageman upon the chance,
Sche leith no peis in the balance,   2380
Bot as hir lyketh forto weie;
The trewe man fulofte aweie
Sche put, which hath hir grace bede,
And set an untrewe in his stede.

Lo, thus blindly the world sche diemeth
In loves cause, as tome siemeth:
I not what othre men wol sein,
Bot I algate am so besein,
And stonde as on amonges alle
Which am out of hir grace falle: 2390
It nedeth take no witnesse,
For sche which seid is the goddesse,
To whether part of love it wende,
Hath sett me for a final ende
The point wherto that I schal holde.
For whan sche hath me wel beholde,
Halvynge of scorn, sche seide thus:
'Thou wost wel that I am Venus,
Which al only my lustes seche;
And wel I wot, thogh thou beseche   2400
Mi love, lustes ben ther none
Whiche I mai take in thi persone;
For loves lust and lockes hore
In chambre acorden neveremore,
And thogh thou feigne a yong corage,
It scheweth wel be the visage
That olde grisel is no fole:
There ben fulmanye yeres stole
With thee and with suche othre mo,
That outward feignen youthe so   2410
And ben withinne of pore assay.
"Min herte wolde and I ne may"
Is noght beloved nou adayes;
Er thou make eny suche assaies
To love, and faile upon the fet,
Betre is to make a beau retret;
For thogh thou myhtest love atteigne,
Yit were it bot an ydel peine,
Whan that thou art noght sufficant
To holde love his covenant.   2420
Forthi tak hom thin herte ayein,
That thou travaile noght in vein,

Wherof my court may be deceived.
I wot and have it wel conceived,
Hou that thi will is good ynowh;
Bot mor behoveth to the plowh,
Wherof the lacketh, as I trowe:
So sitte it wel that thou beknowe
Thi fieble astat, er thou beginne
Thing wher thou miht non ende winne.   2430
What bargain scholde a man assaie,
Whan that him lacketh forto paie?
Mi sone, if thou be wel bethoght,
This toucheth thee; foryet it noght:
The thing is torned into "was";
That which was whilom grene gras,
Is welked hey at time now.
Forthi mi conseil is that thou
Remembre wel hou thou art old.'

Whan Venus hath hir tale told,   2440
And I bethoght was al aboute,
Tho wiste I wel withoute doute,
That ther was no recoverir;
And as a man the blase of fyr
With water quencheth, so ferd I;
A cold me cawhte sodeinly,
For sorwe that myn herte made
Mi dedly face pale and fade
Becam, and swoune I fell to grounde.
And as I lay the same stounde,   2450
Ne fully quik ne fully ded,
Me thoghte I sih tofor myn hed
Cupide with his bowe bent,
And lich unto a parlement,
Which were ordeigned for the nones,
With him cam al the world at ones
Of gentil folk that whilom were
Lovers, I sih hem alle there
Forth with Cupide in sondri routes.

Min yhe and as I caste aboutes,   2460
To knowe among hem who was who,
   I sih wher lusty Youthe tho,
As he which was a capitein,
Tofore alle othre upon the plein
Stod with his route wel begon,
Here hevedes kempt, and therupon
Garlandes noght of o colour,
Some of the lef, some of the flour,
And some of grete perles were;
The newe guise of Beawme there,   2470
With sondri thinges wel devised,
I sih, wherof thei ben queintised.
It was al lust that thei with ferde,
Ther was no song that I ne herde,
Which unto love was touchende;
Of Pan and al that was likende
As in pipinge of melodie
Was herd in thilke compaignie
So lowde, that on every side
It thoghte as al the hevene cride   2480
In such acord and such a soun
Of bombard and of clarion
With cornemuse and schallemele,
That it was half a mannes hele
So glad a noise forto hiere.
And as me thoghte, in this manere
Al freissh I syh hem springe and dance,
And do to love her entendance
After the lust of youthes heste.
Ther was ynowh of joie and feste,   2490
For evere among thei laghe and pleie,
And putten care out of the weie,
That he with hem ne sat ne stod.
And overthis I understod,
So as myn ere it myhte areche,
The moste matiere of her speche
Was al of knyhthod and of armes,

And what it is to ligge in armes
With love, whanne it is achieved.
   Ther was Tristram, which was believed   2500
With bele Ysolde, and Lancelot
Stod with Gunnore, and Galahot
With his ladi, and, as me thoghte,
I syh wher Jason with him broghte
His love, which that Creusa hihte,
And Hercules, which mochel myhte,
Was ther berende his grete mace,
And most of alle in thilke place
He peyneth him to make chiere
With Eolen, which was him diere.   2510
   Theseüs, thogh he were untrewe
To love, as alle wommen knewe,
Yit was he there natheles
With Phedra, whom to love he ches:
Of Grece ek ther was Thelamon,
Which fro the king Lamenedon
At Troie his doghter refte aweie,
Eseonen, as for his preie,
Which take was whan Jason cam
Fro Colchos, and the cite nam   2520
In vengance of the ferste hate;
That made hem after to debate,
Whan Priamus the newe toun
Hath mad. And in avisioun
Me thoghte that I sih also
Ector forth with his brethren tuo;
Himself stod with Pantaselee,
And next to him I myhte se,
Wher Paris stod with faire Eleine,
Which was his joie sovereine;   2530
And Troilus stod with Criseide,
Bot evere among, althogh he pleide,
Be semblant he was hevy chiered,
For Diomede, as him was liered,
Cleymeth to ben his parconner.

And thus full many a bacheler,
A thousend mo than I can sein,
With Yowthe I sih ther wel besein
Forth with here loves glade and blithe.
   And some I sih whiche ofte sithe   2540
Compleignen hem in other wise;
Among the whiche I syh Narcise
And Piramus, that sory were.
The worthy Grek also was there,
Achilles, which for love deide:
Agemenon ek, as men seide,
And Menelay the king also
I syh, with many an other mo,
Which hadden be fortuned sore
In loves cause.
           And overmore   2550
Of wommen in the same cas,
With hem I sih wher Dido was,
Forsake which was with Enee;
And Phillis ek I myhte see,
Whom Demephon deceived hadde;
And Adriagne hir sorwe ladde,
For Theseüs hir soster tok
And hire unkindely forsok.
I sih ther ek among the press
Compleignende upon Hercules   2560
His ferste love Deyanire,
Which sette him afterward afyre:
Medea was there ek and pleigneth
Upon Jason, for that he feigneth,
Withoute cause and tok a newe;
Sche seide, 'Fy on alle untrewe!'
I sih there ek Deÿdamie,
Which hadde lost the compaignie
Of Achilles, whan Diomede
To Troie him fette upon the nede.   2570
   Among these othre upon the grene
I syh also the wofull queene

Cleopatras, which in a cave
With serpentz hath hirself begrave
Alquik, and so sche was totore,
For sorwe of that sche hadde lore
Antonye, which hir love hath be:
And forth with hire I sih Tisbee,
Which on the scharpe swerdes point
For love deide in sory point; 2580
And as myn ere it myhte knowe,
She seide, 'Wo worthe alle slowe!'
The pleignte of Progne and Philomene
Ther herde I what it wolde mene,
How Tereüs of his untrouthe
Undede hem bothe, and that was routhe;
And next to hem I sih Canace,
Which for Machaire hir fader grace
Hath lost, and deide in wofull plit.
And as I sih in my spirit, 2590
Me thoghte amonges othre thus
The doghter of king Priamus,
Polixena, whom Pirrus slowh,
Was there and made sorwe ynowh,
As sche which deide gulteles
For love, and yit was loveles.

And forto take the desport,
I sih there some of other port,
And that was Circes and Calipse,
That cowthen do the mone eclipse, 2600
Of men and change the liknesses,
Of artmagique sorceresses;
Thei hielde in honde manyon,
To love wher thei wolde or non.

Bot above alle that ther were
Of wommen I sih foure there,
Whos name I herde most comended:
Be hem the court stod al amended;
For wher thei comen in presence,
Men deden hem the reverence, 2610

As thogh they hadden be goddesses,
Of al this world or emperesses.
And as me thoghte, an ere I leide,
And herde hou that these othre seide,
'Lo, these ben the foure wyves,
Whos feith was proeved in her lyves:
For in essample of alle goode
With mariage so thei stode,
That fame, which no gret thing hydeth,
Yit in cronique of hem abydeth.'   2620

  Penolope that on was hote,
Whom many a knyht hath loved hote,
Whil that hire lord Ulixes lay
Full many a yer and many a day
Upon the grete siege of Troie:
Bot sche, which hath no worldes joie
Bot only of hire housebonde,
Whil that hir lord was out of londe,
So wel hath kept hir wommanhiede,
That al the world therof tok hiede,   2630
And nameliche of hem in Grece.

  That other womman was Lucrece,
Wif to the Romain Collatin;
And sche constreigned of Tarquin
To thing which was ayein hir wille,
Sche wolde noght hirselven stille,
Bot deide only for drede of schame
In keping of hire goode name,
As sche which was on of the beste.

  The thridde wif was hote Alceste,   2640
Which whanne Ametus scholde dye
Upon his grete maladye,
Sche preide unto the goddes so,
That sche receyveth al the wo
And deide hirself to yive him lif:
Lo, if this were a noble wif!

  The ferthe wif which I ther sih,
I herde of hem that were nyh

Hou sche was cleped Alcione,
Which to Seyix hir lord al one   2650
And to nomo hir body kepte;
And whan sche sih him dreynt, sche lepte
Into the wawes where he swam,
And there a sefoul sche becam,
And with hire wenges him bespradde
For love which to him sche hadde.
    Lo, these foure were tho
Whiche I sih, as me thoghte tho,
Among the grete compaignie
Which Love hadde forto guye: 2660
Bot Youthe, which in special
Of Loves court was mareschal,
So besy was upon his lay,
That he non hiede where I lay
Hath take. And thanne, as I behield,
Me thoghte I sih upon the field,
Where Elde cam a softe pas
Toward Venus, ther as sche was.
With him gret compaignie he ladde,
Bot noght so manye as Youthe hadde: 2670
The moste part were of gret age,
And that was sene in the visage,
And noght forthi, so as thei myhte,
Thei made hem yongly to the sihte:
Bot yit herde I no pipe there
To make noise in mannes ere,
Bot the musette I myhte knowe,
For olde men which souneth lowe,
With harpe and lute and with citole.
The hovedance and the carole,   2680
In such a wise as love hath bede,
A softe pas thei dance and trede;
And with the wommen otherwhile
With sobre chier among thei smyle,
For laghtre was ther non on hyh.
And natheles full wel I syh

That thei the more queinte it made
For love, in whom thei weren glade.
  And there me thoghte I myhte se
The king David with Bersabee,   2690
And Salomon was noght withoute;
Passende an hundred on a route
Of wyves and of concubines,
Juesses bothe and Sarazines,
To him I sih alle entendant:
I not if he was sufficant,
Bot natheles for al his wit
He was attached with that writ
Which love with his hond enseleth,
Fro whom non erthly man appeleth.   2700
And overthis, as for a wonder,
With his leon which he put under,
With Dalida Sampson I knew,
Whos love his strengthe al overthrew.
  I syh there Aristotle also,
Whom that the queene of Grece so
Hath bridled, that in thilke time
Sche made him such a silogime,
That he foryat al his logique;
Ther was non art of his practique,   2710
Thurgh which it mihte ben excluded
That he ne was fully concluded
To love, and dede his obeissance.
And ek Virgile of aqueintance
I sih, wher he the maiden preide,
Which was the doghter, as men seide,
Of th'emperour whilom of Rome;
Sortes and Plato with him come,
So dede Ovide the poete.
I thoghte thanne how love is swete,   2720
Which hath so wise men reclamed,
And was miself the lasse aschamed,
Or forto lese or forto winne
In the meschief that I was inne:

And thus I lay in hope of grace.
 And whan thei comen to the place
Wher Venus stod and I was falle,
These olde men with o vois alle
To Venus preiden for my sake.
And sche, that myhte noght forsake   2730
So gret a clamour as was there,
Let Pite come into hire ere;
And forth withal unto Cupide
Sche preith that he upon his side
Me wolde thurgh his grace sende
Som confort, that I myhte amende,
Upon the cas which is befalle.
And thus for me thei preiden alle
Of hem that weren olde aboute,
And ek some of the yonge route,   2740
Of gentilesse and pure trouthe,
I herde hem telle it was gret routhe
That I withouten help so ferde.
And thus me thoghte I lay and herde.

 Cupido, which may hurte and hele
In loves cause, as for myn hele
Upon the point which him was preid
Cam with Venus, wher I was leid
Swounende upon the grene gras.
And, as me thoghte, anon ther was   2750
On every side so gret presse,
That every lif began to presse,
I wot noght wel hou many score,
Suche as I spak of now tofore,
Lovers, that comen to beholde,
Bot most of hem that weren olde:
Thei stoden there at thilke tyde,
To se what ende schal betyde
Upon the cure of my sotie.
Tho myhte I hiere gret partie   2760
Spekende, and ech his oghne avis

Hath told, on that, an other this:
Bot among alle this I herde,
Thei weren wo that I so ferde,
And seiden that for no riote
An old man scholde noght assote;
For as thei tolden redely,
Ther is in him no cause why,
Bot if he wolde himself benyce;
So were he wel the more nyce.   2770
And thus desputen some of tho,
And some seiden nothing so,
Bot that the wylde loves rage
In mannes lif forberth non age;
Whil ther is oyle forto fyre,
The lampe is lyhtly set afyre,
And is ful hard er it be queynt,
Bot only if it be som seint,
Which god preserveth of his grace.
And thus me thoghte, in sondri place   2780
Of hem that walken up and doun
Ther was diverse opinioun:
And for a while so it laste,
Til that Cupide to the laste,
Forth with his moder full avised,
Hath determined and devised
Unto what point he wol descende.
And al this time I was liggende
Upon the ground tofore his yhen,
And thei that my desese syhen   2790
Supposen noght I scholde live;
Bot he, which wolde thanne yive
His grace, so as it mai be,
This blinde god which mai noght se,
Hath groped til that he me fond;
And as he pitte forth his hond
Upon my body, wher I lay,
Me thoghte a fyri lancegay,
Which whilom thurgh myn herte he caste,

He pulleth oute, and also faste   2800
As this was do, Cupide nam
His weie, I not where he becam,
And so dede al the remenant
Which unto him was entendant,
Of hem that in avision
I hadde a revelacion,
So as I tolde now tofore.
    Bot Venus wente noght therfore,
Ne Genius, whiche thilke time
Abiden bothe faste byme.   2810
And sche which mai the hertes bynde
In loves cause and ek unbinde,
Er I out of mi trance aros,
Venus, which hield a boiste clos,
And wolde noght I scholde deie,
Tok out mor cold than eny keie
An oignement, and in such point
Sche hath my wounded herte enoignt,
My temples and my reins also.
And forth withal sche tok me tho   2820
A wonder mirour forto holde,
In which sche bad me to beholde
And taken hiede of that I syhe;
Wherinne anon myn hertes yhe
I caste, and sih my colour fade,
Myn yhen dymme and al unglade,
Mi chiekes thinne, and al my face
With elde I myhte se deface,
So riveled and so wo besein,
That ther was nothing full ne plein,   2830
I syh also myn heres hore.
Mi will was tho to se nomore
Outwith, for ther was no plesance;
And thanne into my remembrance
I drowh myn olde daies passed,
And as reson it hath compassed,
I made a liknesse of miselve

Unto the sondri monthes twelve,
Wherof the yeer in his astat
Is mad, and stant upon debat,   2840
That lich til other non acordeth.
For who the times wel recordeth,
And thanne at Marche if he beginne,
Whan that the lusti yeer comth inne,
Til Augst be passed and Septembre,
The myhty youthe he may remembre
In which the yeer hath his deduit
Of gras, of lef, of flour, of fruit,
Of corn and of the wyny grape.
And afterward the time is schape   2850
To frost, to snow, to wind, to rein,
Til eft that Mars be come ayein:
The wynter wol no somer knowe,
The grene lef is overthrowe,
The clothed erthe is thanne bare,
Despuiled is the somerfare,
That erst was hete is thanne chele.
  And thus thenkende thoghtes fele,
I was out of mi swoune affraied,
Wherof I sih my wittes straied,   2860
And gan to clepe hem hom ayein.
And whan Resoun it herde sein
That loves rage was aweie,
He cam to me the rihte weie,
And hath remued the sotie
Of thilke unwise fantasie,
Wherof that I was wont to pleigne,
So that of thilke fyri peine
I was mad sobre and hol ynowh.
  Venus behield me than and lowh,   2870
And axeth, as it were in game,
What love was. And I for schame
Ne wiste what I scholde ansuere;
And natheles I gan to swere
That be my trouthe I knew him noght;

116

So ferr it was out of mi thoght,
Riht as it hadde nevere be.
'Mi goode sone,' tho quod sche,
'Now at this time I lieve it wel,
So goth the fortune of my whiel;   2880
Forthi mi conseil is thou leve.'
    'Ma dame,' I seide, 'be your leve,
Ye witen wel, and so wot I,
That I am unbehovely
Your court fro this day forth to serve:
And for I may no thonk deserve,
And also for I am refused,
I preie you to ben excused.
And natheles as for the laste,
Whil that my wittes with me laste,   2890
Touchende mi confession
I axe an absolucion
Of Genius, er that I go.'
The prest anon was redy tho,
And seide, 'Sone, as of thi schrifte
Thou hast ful pardoun and foryifte;
Foryet it thou, and so wol I.'

Amans   'Min holi fader, grant mercy,'
Quod I to him, and to the queene
I fell on knes upon the grene,   2900
And tok my leve forto wende.
Bot sche, that wolde make an ende,
As therto which I was most able,
A peire of bedes blak as sable
Sche tok and heng my necke aboute;
Upon the gaudes al withoute
Was write of gold, *Por reposer*.
'Lo,' thus sche seide, 'John Gower,
Now thou art ate laste cast,
This have I for thin ese cast,   2910
That thou nomore of love sieche.
Bot my will is that thou besieche
And preie hierafter for the pes,

117

And that thou make a plein reles
To love, which takth litel hiede
Of olde men upon the nede,
Whan that the lustes ben aweie:
Forthi to thee nys bot o weie,
In which let Reson be thi guide;
For he may sone himself misguide,   2920
That seth noght the peril tofore.
Mi sone, be wel war therfore,
And kep the sentence of my lore
And tarie thou mi court nomore,
Bot go ther vertu moral duelleth,
Wher ben thi bokes, as men telleth,
Whiche of long time thou hast write.
For this I do thee wel to wite,
If thou thin hele wolt pourchace,
Thou miht noght make suite and chace,   2930
Wher that the game is nought pernable;
It were a thing unresonable,
A man to be so overseie.
Forthi tak hiede of that I seie;
For in the lawe of my comune
We be noght schape to comune,
Thiself and I, nevere after this.
Now have y seid al that ther is
Of love as for thi final ende:
Adieu, for I mot fro the wende.   2940
    And gret wel Chaucer whan ye mete,
As mi disciple and mi poete:
For in the floures of his youthe
In sondri wise, as he wel couthe,
Of ditees and of songes glade,
The whiche he for mi sake made,
The lond fulfild is overal:
Wherof to him in special
Above alle othre I am most holde.
Forthi now in hise daies olde   2950
Thow schalt him telle this message,

That he upon his latere age,
To sette an ende of alle his werk,
As he which is myn owne clerk,
Do make his testament of love,
As thou hast do thi schrifte above,
So that mi court it mai recorde.'

   'Madame, I can me wel acorde,'
Quod I, 'to telle as ye me bidde.'
And with that word it so betidde,   2960
Out of my sihte al sodeynly,
Enclosed in a sterred sky,
Up to the hevene Venus straghte,
And I my rihte weie cawhte,
Hom fro the wode and forth I wente,
Wher as with al myn hole entente,
Thus with mi bedes upon honde,
For hem that trewe love fonde
I thenke bidde whil I lyve
Upon the poynt which I am schryve.   2970

   He which withinne dayes sevene
This large world forth with the hevene
Of his eternal providence
Hath mad, and thilke intelligence
In mannes soule resonable
Enspired to himself semblable,
Wherof the man of his feture
Above alle erthly creature
After the soule is immortal,
To thilke lord in special,   2980
As he which is of alle thinges
The creatour, and of the kinges
Hath the fortunes upon honde,
His grace and mercy forto fonde
Upon mi bare knees I preye,
That he my worthi king conveye,
Richard by name the Secounde,
In whom hath evere yit be founde

Justice medled with pite,
Largesce forth with charite.   2990
In his persone it mai be schewed
What is a king to be wel thewed,
Touchinge of pite namely:
For he yit nevere unpitously
Ayein the liges of his lond,
For no defaute which he fond,
Thurgh cruelte vengaunce soghte;
And thogh the worldes chaunce in broghte
Of infortune gret debat,
Yit was he not infortunat: 3000
For he which the fortune ladde,
The hihe god, him overspradde
Of his justice, and kepte him so,
That his astat stood evere mo
Sauf, as it oghte wel to be;
Lich to the sonne in his degree,
Which with the clowdes up alofte
Is derked and bischadewed ofte,
But hou so that it trowble in th'eir,
The sonne is evere briht and feir,   3010
Withinne himself and noght empeired:
Althogh the weder be despeired,
The hed planete is not to wite.
Mi worthi prince, of whom I write,
Thus stant he with himselve clier,
And doth what lith in his power
Not only hier at hom to seke
Love and acord, but outward eke,
As he that save his poeple wolde.
So ben we alle wel beholde   3020
To do service and obeyssaunce
To him, which of his heyh suffraunce
Hath many a gret debat appesed,
To make his lige men ben esed;
Wherfore that his croniqe schal
For evere be memorial

To the loenge of that he doth.
For this wot every man in soth,
What king that so desireth pes,
He takth the weie which Crist ches: 3030
And who that Cristes weies sueth,
It proveth wel that he eschueth
The vices and is vertuous,
Wherof he mot be gracious
Toward his god and acceptable.
And so to make his regne stable,
With al the wil that I mai yive
I preie and schal whil that I live,
As I which in subjeccioun
Stonde under the proteccioun,   3040
And mai miselven not bewelde,
What for seknesse and what for elde,
Which I receyve of goddes grace.
But thogh me lacke to purchace
Mi kinges thonk as by decerte,
Yit the simplesce of mi poverte
Unto the love of mi ligance
Desireth forto do plesance:
And for this cause in myn entente
This povere bok heer I presente   3050
Unto his hihe worthinesse,
Write of my simple besinesse,
So as seknesse it suffre wolde.
And in such wise as I ferst tolde,
Whan I this bok began to make,
In som partie it mai be take
As for to lawhe and forto pleye;
And forto loke in other weye,
It mai be wisdom to the wise:
So that somdel for good aprise   3060
And eek somdel for lust and game
I have it mad, as thilke same
Which axe forto ben excused,
That I no rethoriqe have used

Upon the forme of eloquence,
For that is not of mi science;
But I have do my trewe peyne
With rude wordes and with pleyne
To speke of thing which I have told.
   But now that I am feble and old, 3070
And to the worschipe of mi king
In love above alle other thing
That I this bok have mad and write,
Mi muse doth me forto wite
That it is to me for the beste
Fro this day forth to take reste,
That I nomore of love make.
But he which hath of love his make
It sit him wel to singe and daunce,
And do to love his entendance 3080
In songes bothe and in seyinges
After the lust of his pleyinges,
For he hath that he wolde have:
But where a man schal love crave
And faile, it stant al otherwise.
In his proverbe seith the wise,
Whan game is best, is best to leve:
And thus forthi my fynal leve,
Withoute makyng eny more,
I take now for evere more 3090
Of love and of his dedly hele,
Which no phisicien can hele.
For his nature is so divers,
That it hath evere som travers
Or of to moche or of to lite,
That fully mai noman delyte,
But if him lacke or that or this.
But thilke love which that is
Withinne a mannes herte affermed,
And stant of charite confermed, 3100
That love is of no repentaile;
For it ne berth no contretaile,

Which mai the conscience charge,
But it is rather of descharge,
And meedful heer and overal.
Forthi this love in special
Is good for every man to holde,
And who that resoun wol beholde,
Al other lust is good to daunte:
Which thing the hihe god us graunte   3110
Forth with the remenant of grace
So that of hevene in thilke place
Wher resteth love and alle pes,
Oure joye mai ben endeles.

Epistola super huius opusculi sui complementum Iohanni Gower a quodam philosopho transmissa.

Quam cinxere freta, Gower, tua carmina leta
Per loca discreta canit Anglia laude repleta.
Carminis Athleta, satirus, tibi, siue Poeta,
Sit laus completa quo gloria stat sine meta.

'Peace' (*from the verses addressed to Henry IV*)

FOR vein honour or for the worldes good
Thei that whilom the stronge werres made,   100
Wher be thei now? Bethenk wel in thi mod.
The day is goon, the nyght is derk and fade,
Her crualte, which mad hem thanne glade,
Thei sorwen now, and yit have noght the more;
The blod is schad, which no man mai restore.

The werre is modir of the wronges alle;
It sleth the prest in holi chirche at masse,
Forlith the maide and doth hire flour to falle.
The werre makth the grete citee lasse,
And doth the lawe his reules overpasse.   110
There is no thing wherof meschef mai growe
Which is noght caused of the werre, y trowe.

The werre bringth in poverte at hise hieles,
Wherof the comon poeple is sore grieved;
The werre hath set his cart on thilke whieles
Wher that fortune mai noght be believed.
For whan men wene best to have achieved,
Ful ofte it is al newe to beginne:
The werre hath no thing siker, thogh he winne.

Forthi, my worthi prince, in Cristes halve,   120
As for a part whos feith thou hast to guide,
Ley to this olde sor a newe salve,
And do the werre awei, what so betide:
Pourchace pes, and set it be thi side,
And suffre noght thi poeple be devoured,
So schal thi name evere after stonde honoured.

If eny man be now or evere was
Ayein the pes thi preve counseillour,
Let god ben of thi counseil in this cas,
And put awei the cruel werreiour.   130
For god, which is of man the creatour,
He wolde noght men slowe his creature
Withoute cause of dedly forfeture.

.   .   .   .

More light it is to kepe than to make;
Bot that we founden mad tofore the hond
We kepe noght, bot lete it lightly slake   220
The pes of Crist hath altobroke his bond,
We reste ourselve and soeffrin every lond
To slen ech other as thing undefendid:
So stant the werre, and pes is noght amendid.

.   .   .   .

Noght only to my king of pes y write,
Bot to these othre princes cristene alle,   380
That ech of hem his oghne herte endite,
And see the werre er more mischief falle:
Sette ek the rightful pope uppon his stalle,
Kepe charite, and draugh pite to honde,
Maintene law, and so the pes schal stonde.

Finis.

THREE BALADES

XXXIV

1. SAINT Valentin l'amour et la nature
   De toutz oiseals ad en governement;
   Dont chascun d'eaux semblable a sa mesure
   Une compaigne honeste a son talent
   Eslist tout d'un acord et d'un assent:
   Pour celle soule laist a covenir
   Toutes les autres, car nature aprent,
   U li coers est, le corps falt obeïr.

2. Ma doulce dame, ensi jeo vous assure
   Qe jeo vous ai eslieu semblablement;   10
   Sur toutes autres estes a dessure
   De mon amour si tresentierement,
   Qe riens y falt par quoi joiousement
   De coer et corps jeo vous voldrai servir:
   Car de reson c'est une experiment,
   U li coers est, le corps falt obeïr.

3. Pour remembrer jadis celle aventure
   De Alceone et Ceïx ensement,
   Com dieus muoit en oisel lour figure,
   Ma volenté serroit tout tielement,   20
   Qe sanz envie et danger de la gent
   Nous porroions ensemble par loisir
   Voler tout francs en nostre esbatement:
   U li coers est, le corps falt obeïr.

4. Ma belle oisel, vers qui mon pensement
   S'en vole ades sanz null contretenir,
   Pren cest escript, car jeo sai voirement,
   U li coers est, le corps falt obeïr.

XXXV

1. SAINT Valentin plus qe null Emperour
   Ad parlement et convocacion
   Des toutz oiseals, qui vienont a son jour,
   U la compaigne prent son compaignon
   En droit amour; mais par comparison
   D'ascune part ne puiss avoir la moie:
   Qui soul remaint ne poet avoir grant joie.

2. Com la fenix souleine est au sojour
   En Arabie celle regioun,
   Ensi ma dame en droit de son amour   10
   Souleine maint, ou si jeo vuill ou noun,
   N'ad cure de ma supplicacion,
   Sique d'amour ne sai troever la voie:
   Qui soul remaint ne poet avoir grant joie.

3. O com nature est pleine de favour
   A ceos oiseals q'ont lour eleccion!
   O si jeo fuisse en droit de mon atour
   En ceo soul cas de lour condicioun!
   Plus poet nature qe ne poet resoun,
   En mon estat tresbien le sente et voie: 20
   Qui soul remaint ne poet avoir grant joie.

4. Chascun Tarcel gentil ad sa falcoun,
   Mais j'ai faili de ceo q'avoir voldroie:
   Ma dame, c'est le fin de mon chançoun,
   Qui soul remaint ne poet avoir grant joie.

XXXVI

1. POUR comparer ce jolif temps de Maii,
   Jeo le dirrai semblable a Paradis;
   Car lors chantont et merle et papegai,
   Les champs sont vert, les herbes sont floris,
   Lors est nature dame du paiis;

Dont Venus poignt l'amant au tiel assai,
Q'encontre amour n'est qui poet dire Nai.

2. Qant tout ceo voi et qe jeo penserai
   Coment nature ad tout le mond suspris,
   Dont pour le temps se fait minote et gai,   10
   Et jeo des autres sui soulein horpris,
   Com cil qui sanz amie est vrais amis,
   N'est pas mervaile lors si jeo m'esmai,
   Q'encontre amour n'est qui poet dire Nai.

3. En lieu de Rose urtie cuillerai,
   Dont mes chapeals ferrai par tiel devis,
   Qe toute joie et confort jeo lerrai,
   Si celle soule, en qui j'ai mon coer mis,
   Selonc le point qe j'ai sovent requis,
   Ne deigne alegger les griefs mals qe j'ai;   20
   Q'encontre amour n'est qui poet dire Nai.

4. Pour pité querre et pourchacer mercis,
   Va t'en, balade, u jeo t'envoierai;
   Q'ore en certein jeo l'ai tresbien apris,
   Q'encontre amour n'est qui poet dire Nai.

EXTRACTS FROM THE *MIROUR DE L'OMME*

(i) *The Marriage of Sin's Daughters* (ll. 841–948)

Comment les sept files du Pecché vindront vers leur mariage, et de leur arrai et de leur chiere.

CHASCUNE soer endroit du soy
L'un apres l'autre ove son conroi
Vint en sa guise noblement,
Enchivalchant par grant desroy;
Mais ce n'estoit sur palefroy,
Ne sur les mules d'orient:
Orguil qui vint primerement
S'estoit monté moult fierement
Sur un lioun, q'aler en coy
Ne volt pour nul chastiement,   850
Ainz salt sur la menue gent,
Du qui tous furont en effroy.

    Du selle et frein quoy vous dirray,
Du mantellet ou d'autre array?
Trestout fuist plain du queinterie;
Car unques prée flouriz en maii
N'estoit au reguarder si gay
Des fleurs, comme ce fuist du perrie:
Et sur son destre poign saisie
Une aigle avoit, que signefie   860
Qu'il trestous autres a l'essay
Volt surmonter de s'estutye.
Ensi vint a la reverie
La dame dont parlé vous ay.

    Puis vint Envye en son degré,
Q'estoit dessur un chien monté,
Et sur son destre poign portoit
Un espervier q'estoit mué:
La face ot moult descolouré

Et pale des mals que pensoit, 870
Et son mantell dont s'affoubloit
Du purpre au droit devis estoit
Ove cuers ardans bien enbroudé,
Et entre d'eux, qui bien seoit,
Du serpent langues y avoit
Par tout menuement poudré.
　　Apres Envye vint suiant
Sa soer dame Ire enchivalchant
Moult fierement sur un sengler,
Et sur son poign un cock portant. 880
Soulaine vint, car attendant
Avoit ne sergant n'escuier;
La cote avoit du fin acier,
Et des culteals plus d'un millier
Q'au coste luy furont pendant:
Trop fuist la dame a redouter,
Tous s'en fuiont de son sentier,
Et la lessont passer avant.
　　Dessur un asne lent et lass
Enchivalchant le petit pass 890
Puis vint Accidie loign derere,
Et sur son poign pour son solas
Tint un huan ferm par un las:
Si ot toutdis pres sa costiere
Sa couche faite en sa litiere;
N'estoit du merriem ne de piere,
Ainz fuist de plom de halt en bass.
Si vint au feste en tieu maniere,
Mais aulques fuist de mate chere,
Pour ce q'assetz ne dormi pas. 900
　　Dame Avarice apres cela
Vint vers le feste et chivalcha
Sur un baucan qui voit toutdis
Devers la terre, et pour cela
Nulle autre beste tant prisa:
Si ot sur l'un des poigns assis
Un ostour qui s'en vait toutdis

Pour proye, et dessur l'autre ot mis
Un merlot q'en larcine va.
Des bources portoit plus que dis,   910
Que tout de l'orr sont replenis:
Moult fuist l'onour q'om le porta.
　　Bien tost apres il me sovient
Que dame Gloutonie vient,
Que sur le lou s'est chivalché,
Et sur son poign un coufle tient,
Q'a sa nature bien avient;
Si fist porter pres sa costée
Beau cop de vin envessellé:
N'ot guaire deux pass chivalchée,   920
Quant Yveresce luy survient,
Saisist le frein, si l'ad mené,
Et dist de son droit heritée
Que cel office a luy partient.
　　Puis vi venir du queinte atour
La dame q'ad fait maint fol tour,
C'est Leccherie la plus queinte:
En un manteal de fol amour
Sist sur le chievre q'est lecchour,
En qui luxure n'est restreinte,   930
Et sur son poign soutz sa constreinte
Porte un colomb; dont meint et meinte
Pour l'aguarder s'en vont entour.
Du beal colour la face ot peinte,
Oels vairs riantz, dont mainte enpeinte
Ruoit au fole gent entour.
　　Et d'autre part sans nul demeure
Le Siecle vint en mesme l'eure,
Et c'estoit en le temps joly
Du Maii, quant la deesce Nature   940
Bois, champs et prées de sa verdure
Reveste, et l'oisel font leur cry,
Chantant deinz ce buisson flori,
Que point l'amie ove son amy:
Lors cils que vous nomay desseure

Les noces font, comme je vous dy:
Moult furont richement servy
Sanz point, sanz reule et sanz mesure.

(ii) *A prayer to the Virgin* (ll. 29905–end of MS.)

O DAME, pour la remembrance
De ton honour et ta plesance
Tes nouns escrivre je voldrai;
Car j'ay en toy tiele esperance,
Que tu m'en fretz bonne alleggance,
Si humblement te nomerai.   29910
Pour ce ma langue enfilerai,
Et tout mon cuer obeierai,
Solonc ma povre sufficance
Tes nouns benoitz j'escriveray,
Au fin que je par ce porray,
Ma dame, avoir ta bienvuillance.
    O mere et vierge sanz lesure,
O la treshumble creature,
Joye des angles gloriouse,
O merciable par droiture.   29920
Restor de nostre forsfaiture,
Fontaine en grace plentevouse,
O belle Olive fructuouse,
Palme et Cipresse preciouse,
O de la mer estoille pure,
O cliere lune esluminouse,
O amiable, o amourouse
Du bon amour qui toutdis dure.
    O rose sanz espine dite,
Odour de balsme, o mirre eslite,   29930
O fleur du lys, o turturelle,
O vierge de Jesse confite,
Commencement de no merite,
O dieu espouse, amye, ancelle,
O debonaire columbelle,

Sur toutes belles la plus belle,
O gem*m*e, o fine Margarite,
Mere de mercy l'en t'appelle,
Tu es de ciel la fenestrelle
Et porte a paradis p*ar*fite.   29940
      O gloriouse mere dée,
Vierge des vierges renom*m*ée,
De toy le fils dieu deigna nestre;
O temple de la deité,
Essample auci de chastité. . . .

    .   .   .   .   .   •

EXTRACTS FROM *VOX CLAMANTIS*

(i) *The Peasants' Revolt* (i. 783–816)

WATTE vocat, cui Thomme venit, neque Symme retardat,
Bette que Gibbe simul Hykke venire iubent:
Colle furit, quem Geffe iuuat, nocumenta parantes,
Cum quibus ad dampnum Wille coire vouet.
Grigge rapit, dum Dawe strepit, comes est quibus Hobbe,
Lorkyn et in medio non minor esse putat:
Hudde ferit, quos Iudde terit, dum Tebbe minatur,
Iakke domos que viros vellit et ense necat: 790
Hogge suam pompam vibrat, dum se putat omni
Maiorem Rege nobilitate fore:
Balle propheta docet, quem spiritus ante malignus
Edocuit, que sua tunc fuit alta scola.
Talia quam plures furias per nomina noui,
Que fuerant alia pauca recordor ego:
Sepius exclamant monstrorum vocibus altis,
Atque modis variis dant variare tonos.
    Quidam sternutant asinorum more ferino,
Mugitus quidam personuere boum;   800
Quidam porcorum grunnitus horridiores
Emittunt, que suo murmure terra tremit:
Frendet aper spumans, magnos facit atque tumultus,
Et quiritat verres auget et ipse sonos;
Latratusque ferus vrbis compresserat auras,
Dumque canum discors vox furibunda volat.
Vulpis egens vlulat, lupus et versutus in altum
Conclamat, que suos conuocat ipse pares;
Nec minus in sonitu concussit garrulus ancer
Aures, que subito fossa dolore pauent: 810
Bombizant vaspe, sonus est horrendus eorum,
Nullus et examen dinumerare potest:
Conclamant pariter hirsuti more leonis,
Omneque fit peius quod fuit ante malum.
Ecce rudis clangor, sonus altus, fedaque rixa,
Vox ita terribilis non fuit vlla prius. . . .

(ii) *Fraud* (v. 735–86)

Postquam dixit de potencia Vsure, iam de Fraudis subtilitate dicere intendit, que de communi consilio quasi omnibus et singulis in emendo et vendendo ea que sunt agenda procurat et subtiliter disponit.

Ista soror grauia parat, altera set grauiora,
Nam stat communis omnibus ipsa locis:
Quo tamen Vsura pergit Fraus vadit et illa,
Vna viam querit, altera complet opus.
Vrbibus Vsura tantum manet hiis sociata
Quorum thesaurus nescit habere pares;   740
Set Fraus ciuiles perstat communis ad omnes,
Consulit et cunctis viribus ipsa suis:
Clam sua facta facit, nam quem plus decipit ipsa,
Ipse prius sentit quam videt inde malum.
    Stans foris ante fores proclamat Fraus iuuenilis
Merces diuersas, quicquid habere velis.
Quot celi stelle, tot dicet nomina rerum,
Huius et istius, et trahit atque vocat:
Quos nequit ex verbis, tractu compellit inire,
'Hic,' ait, 'est quod vos queritis, ecce veni.'   750
Sic apprenticius plebem clamore reducit,
Ad secreta doli quando magister adest:
Dum Fraus namque vetus componit verba dolosa,
Incircumventus nullus abire potest:
Si sapiens intrat, Fraus est sapiencior illo,
Et si stultus init, stulcior inde redit.
    Ad precium duplum Fraus ponit singula, dicens
Sic, 'Ita Parisius Flandria siue dedit.'
Quod minus est in re suplent iurancia verba,
Propter denarium vulnerat ipsa deum;   760
Nam nichil in Cristo membrorum tunc remanebit,
Dum iuramentis Fraus sua lucra petit.
Hac set in arte tamen nos sepe domos fore plenas
Cernimus, et proprium nil domus ipsa tenet:
Sicque per ypocrisim ciuis perquirit honorem,

135

Quo genuflexa procul plebs valedicat ei:
Accidit vnde sibi quasi furtim maior vt ipse
Astat in vrbe sua, qui minor omnibus est.
Set cum tempus erit quo singula nuda patebunt,
Dedecus euertit quod decus ante fuit;   770
Nam cum quisque suum repetit, tunc coruus amictus
Alterius pennis nudus vt ante volat.
　　Fraus et ab vrbe venit campestres querere lanas,
Ex quibus in stapula post parat acta sua.
Numquid vina petit Fraus que Vasconia gignit?
Hoc dicunt populi rite nocere sibi:
Fraus manet in doleo, trahit et vult vendere vinum,
Sepeque de veteri conficit ipsa nouum.
Fraus eciam pannos vendet, quos lumine fusco
Cernere te faciet, tu magis inde caue: 780
Discernat tactus, vbi fallunt lumina visus,
Ne te pannificus fraudet in arte dolus.
Absit enim species quis vendat Fraude negante,
Dumque suis mixtis dat veterata nouis;
Decimat in lance sibi, partem sepeque sextam
Pondere subtili Fraus capit ipsa sibi.

(iii) *The creation of Man* (vii. 545–66)

　　Stat formatus homo, miratur seque suosque
Gestus, et nescit quid sit et ad quid homo:
Corporis officium miratur, membra moueri,
Artificesque manus articulosque pedum.
Artus distendit, dissoluit brachia, palmis
Corporis attractat singula membra sui: 550
In se quid cernit sese miratur, et ipsam
Quam gerit effigiem non videt esse suam:
Miratur faciem terre variasque figuras,
Et quia non nouit nomina, nescit eas.
Erexit vultus, os sublimauit in altum,
Se rapit ad superos, spiritus vnde fuit:
Miratur celi speciem formamque rotundam,

136

Sidereos motus stelliferasque domos:
Stat nouus attonitus hospes secumque reuoluit,
Quid sibi que cernit corpora tanta velint.   560
Noticiamque tamen illi natura ministrat;
Quod sit homo, quod sunt ista creata videt:
Quod sit ad humanos vsus hic conditus orbis,
Quod sit ei proprius mundus, et ipse dei.
Ardet in auctoris illius sensus amorem,
Iamque recognouit quid sit amare deum.

(iv) *Man the Microcosm* (vii. 637–60)

O pietas domini, qualisque potencia, quanta
Gracia, que tantum fecerat esse virum!
Vir sapit angelicis cum cetibus, vnde supremum
Esse creatorem noscit in orde deum: 640
Sentit et audit homo, gustat, videt, ambulat, vnde
Nature speciem fert animalis homo:
Cum tamen arboribus homo crescit, et optinet esse
In lapidum forma proprietate sua:
Sic minor est mundus homo, qui fert singula solus
Soli solus homo dat sacra vota deo.
Est homo qui mundus de iure suo sibi mundum
Subdit, et in melius dirigit inde status:
Si tamen inmundus est, que sut singula mundi
Ledit, et in peius omne refregit opus: 650
Vt vult ipse suum proprio regit ordine mundum,
Si bonus ipse, bonum, si malus ipse, malum.
Qui minor est mundus, fert mundo maxima dampna,
Ex inmundiciis si cadat ipse reus:
Qui minor est mundus, si non inmunda recidat,
Cuncta suo mundi crimine lesa grauat:
Qui minor est mundus homo, si colat omnipotentem,
Rebus in humanis singula munda parit:
Qui minor est mundus, si iura dei meditetur,
Grande sibi regnum possidet ipse poli.   660

(v) *Amor Patriae* (vii. 1289–1302)

Singula que dominus statuit sibi regna per orbem,
Que magis in Cristi nomie signa gerunt,   1290
Diligo, set propriam super omnia diligo terram,
In qua principium duxit origo meum.
Quicquid agant alie terre, no subruor inde,
Dum tamen ipse foris sisto remotus eis;
Patria set iuuenem que me suscepit alumpnum,
Partibus in cuius semper adhero manens,
Hec si quid patitur, mea viscera compaciuntur,
Nec sine me dampna ferre valebit ea:
Eius in aduersis de pondere sum quasi versus;
Si perstet, persto, si cadit illa, cado.   1300
Que magis ergo grauant presenti tempore, saltem
Vt dicunt alii, scismata plango michi.

NOTES

I

Love and the lover; his plight and his shrift
(*CA*, i. 1–288)

HEADPIECES in Latin elegiacs appear throughout the poem, but only the first two are reproduced in these selections. Sometimes (as in these two sets) they include images and ideas not precisely reproduced in the English verses. The oxymoron of ll. vii–viii is repeated from *Vox Clamantis*, v, c. 2, where it is developed at length; cf. *Roman de la Rose*, 4292–330 (= *Romaunt*, 4703–50). *Natura naturans*, l. i is a scholastic phrase: (*Summa Theologica*, i. 66, i. 2; ii. 85. 6: see Bennett, *The Parlement of Foules* (1957), p. 195, n. 1, and Fisher, *John Gower*, p. 193).

1–10. The reference is primarily to the themes of discord in society which he has treated in the Prologue; there he concludes with the wish for some such a singer as Arion, who brought 'lords and commons' into love and harmony:

> And if ther were such on now
> Which cowthe harpe as he tho dede
> He myhte availe in many a stede
> To make a pes wher now is hate;
> (Prol. 1072–5)

cf. *Mirour*, 22915 ff.; the image of the ruler as a luteplayer who can tune the strings of the state reappears in Nicolas of Cusa, *De concordantia catholica* (cit. R. Klibansky, *Saturn and Melancholy* (1964), p. 119). But 'my writinges' refers more generally to the *Mirour* and *Vox Clamantis*, concerned as they were with strife and discord in the body politic. The mere mention of these works here must affect our view of the narrator's *persona*: he is evidently no longer in his 'lusti youthe'.

18–26. Cf. *Roman de Troie*, 18443–9:

> C'est devié lor fait Achillès,
> Se il mesfait, qu'en puet il mais,
> Quant cil li tout sen e mesure,
> Qui ne guarde lei ne dreiture,
> Noblece, honesté ne parage?

Qui est qui vers Amors est sage?
Ço n'est il pas ne ne puet estre;

and *Troilus and Criseyde*, i. 230 (and with l. 31, cf. ib. 238).

21. *natheles* seems to require the unusual sense of 'indeed, moreover':
cf. *CA*, v. 5779 below (VII).

37. 'wheresoever it pleases him to strike' (or 'apply himself').

47. The blindness of love and its disregard of reason is a recurrent
theme: cf. e.g., iii. 155 f., 1465 ff., and esp. v. 1412 ff., where Cupid is
described as blind to Reason when he embraced Venus his mother: 'Thus
was he blind, and sche unwys'; see also *VC*, v. 147 ff. For the iconology
of the theme see E. Panofsky, *Studies in Iconology* (1939), c. iv.

99 f. The sentence is left unfinished in a kind of aposiopesis: cf. iv.
3201 (VI), vi. 1796 ff. and *Mirour*, 89 n.

109. *forfare*: 'tired out with wandering'. The weariness of the narrator-
dreamer is a regular feature of love- and vision-literature: cf. e.g., *Piers
Plowman* B. Prol. 7; *House of Fame*, 115. On the force of *for-* see M. L.
Samuels, *English Studies*, xxxvi (1955), 310–13, and T. F. Mustanoja,
A Middle English Syntax, i (1960), 382, 562.

115. *al myn one*: 'al by myself'. The poss. pron. in such phrases has re-
placed the earlier dat. pron. which was added to *one* ('alone') for emphasis.

139 ff. The *locus classicus* for the shooting of the fiery dart of love is the
Roman de la Rose, 872 ff., 1681 ff. (= 885, 1715 in Chaucer's *Romaunt*),
which Gower certainly knew. Cf. *LGW*, F. 226 ff.

168 f. The conception of a court of love, in which the lover petitions
for grace, recurs throughout the poem: e.g. ii. 39–44, 237–54; iii. 702–6;
v. 4864–7; viii. 2342 ff., 2454 ff. (see VIII, p. 105 above). It is as old as the
Pervigilium Veneris (*Iussit* [*sc.* Venus] *Hyblaeis tribunal stare diva floribus/
Praeses ipsa iura dicit*, 49–50). See also Rolland, *Court of Venus* (S.T.S.
1884), p. xv.

178. *world*: 'fortune' hence 'wheel': cf. v. 3251 (VI). Cf. Prol. 383: 'But
every clerk his herte leith [To kepe his worlde in special', and v. 3637. For
other senses of *world* in Gower, see C. S. Lewis, *Studies in Words* (1967), 9.

196. Genius's role in *CA* is markedly different from that in *VC*, where,
as in the *Roman*, he represents generation and is indifferent to morality.
But it is from the *Roman* that the conception of sins against Love derives:
see Brusendorff, *The Chaucer Tradition*, p. 140, n. 2.

205–6. *Benedicite* [*fili mi*] would be the opening words of a priest
hearing confession, and the penitent would reply *Domine*: cf. 215 and
iv. 1222 (IV below).

225. *my schrifte oppose*: 'examine [cf. L. *opponere*] my confession by asking me questions.' Cf. 'The mynister should not be compelled to *appose* and examine the penitent' (cit. *OED* s.v. *appose*, v¹, s.a. 1558).

232. *tome*. The combination indicates that the stress is to be placed on *to*: cf. *CT*, A. 671–2 and *The Owl and the Nightingale*, 1671–2 (*come*: *tome*). Cf. also *bime*: *time CA*, iv. 1423–4 (IV below).

242 ff. For the elaborate analysis of vices as part of confessional practice, cf. *The Parson's Tale* (*CT*, I, *2da pars Penitencie*, etc.), *Piers Plowman* B, V passim, and Dunbar's *Tabill of Confession* (see *Devotional Pieces* . . . ed. Bennett, STS, Third Series 23, 1949, p. 1). The detail and deliberation of the questions and answers throughout the *Confessio* conform to the precept that confession should be 'true: of thy propre synnes, hole: spedefull: ofte sure: manerly: voluntarely: clere: wyth suche deliberacyon that it may playnly be understande, and with so grete contrycyon that it may make the sory' (*The Sarum Prymer*, ed. of 1538). The Sarum form of confession also indicates how the penitent would confess himself guilty of the seven deadly sins, in the various branches. Gower himself alludes to the technique in *Mirour*, 6128–9: 'Comment serront ses mals guaris / Quant confesser ne sciet ses mals?'; cf. also *Mirour*, 14845–15096.

The deadly sins are similarly defined with reference to love—and with support from philosophical and scriptural texts—in Antoine de la Sale's *Petit Jehan de Saintré* (1456).[1]

271. *nowlher text neglose*: 'neither in text nor commentary', i.e. 'no-where'.

II

The tale of Florent (i. 1407–1861)

The confessor states that he found this *exemplum* of the virtue of humility in love in a 'cronique' (i. 1404)—a term that Gower uses for various sources, usually identifiable.[2] But no specific source for the story or for its analogue in the Wife of Bath's Tale has been found, though the themes of 'the loathly lady' and the *fier baiser* or daring kiss that breaks a spell are widespread.[3] Chaucer gives the tale an Arthurian setting (also

[1] Unlike Gower, La Sale includes *luxuria* (lechery) in the sins, defining it as consorting with common women.

[2] e.g. i. 759, where the source is Hegesippus.

[3] Some of the analogues are discussed by S. Eisner, *A Tale of Wonder* (Wexford, 1957). The ME 'Weddynge of Sir Gawen and Dame Ragnell' and 'Marriage of Sir Gawain' are printed in *Sources and Analogues of the Canterbury Tales* (1941), pp. 233 ff., with some bibliography; see also *Arthurian Literature in the Middle Ages*,

found in the 'Weddynge of Sir Gawen'; see p. 141, n. 3 above) whereas in Gower the lady is a daughter of a king of Sicily, and Florent[ius][1] is nephew to an emperor, identified in the Latin marginal gloss as Claudus. Gower's presentation and emphasis differ from Chaucer's in many other particulars. His hero is in jeopardy through fortune, not because of his rape of a maiden; and there is a different reason for female revenge. His 'gentilesse' is tested, and exemplified, but never questioned; for a discourse on 'gentilesse' similar to the Wife of Bath's we must turn to iv. 2200 ff. or *Mirour*, 17329 ff. Gower, again, mentions no time limit—in Chaucer it is a year and a day. There is no dance, as in Chaucer, of damsels who mysteriously vanish. Gower's 'vecke' knows the hero's name and his dilemma and what the people of the castle will say, and she obtains his pledge before giving him the answer. Most important, the issue is one of love as well as sovereignty (l. 1847). Other differences are self-evident; some are the subject of lively comment by T. Silverstein: 'The Wife of Bath and the Rhetoric of Enchantment', *Modern Philology*, lviii (1961), 153–73; see also M. Schlauch, 'The marital dilemma', *PMLA*, lxi (1946), 416–34.

Gower, in effect, describes two critical choices, the second (ll. 1811 ff.) having no equivalent in Chaucer; and he dwells on the release afforded by the hero's final unreserved acceptance of the full implications of his knightly bond. Chaucer on the other hand emphasizes the ultimate obedience of the wife to the husband (*CT*, D. 1255–6) and the triumph of his essential 'courtesye'; he ignores the motif of the spell.

The tale happily illustrates some of Gower's preoccupations and favourite devices, e.g. the use of antithetical balance to symbolize inner conflict and indeterminacy (1569–71, 1708; cf. i. 2336, etc.); the solitary character of hero or heroine (1523; cf. iv. 1295); the quiet pregnant

ed. R. S. Loomis (1959), pp. 501–4. The fourteenth-century *Saga of Hrolf Kraki*, preserves an interesting and concise version:

[King Helgi is in bed when he hears a faint knock at the door. He admits a poor bedraggled creature who begs to sleep beside him 'for my life is at stake']. 'Now she did so, and the king turned himself from her. A lamp burned in the house, and after a time he looked over his shoulder at her; then he perceived that there lay a woman so fair of face that he seemed never before to have beheld her like for beauty; she wore a silk kirtle. He turned speedily towards her then, and joyfully ...' (tr. Stella Mills). He has thus freed her from her stepmother's curse and now insists on 'a hasty marriage' the fruit of which is a daughter whom the elfin wife brings to the king before passing out of his sight for ever. E. R. Curtius, *European Literature in the Latin Middle Ages* (tr. Trask), p. 104, notes the survival of such transformation scenes in dream-literature as late as Balzac, but does not mention Gower's treatment.

[1] This Latin form, found in the marginal gloss, also appears in *The Taming of the Shrew*, I. ii. 69: 'Be she as foul as was Florentius' love. . . .'

phrase (e.g. 'we ben bothe on', 1793). It also shows his dialogue and description at their crispest: the frouncing of the 'olde mones' brow, her proffer of a body 'lich unto the wollesak', Florent lifting up his 'wofull heved'—these are all characteristic touches.

1411. *Florent.* The name is not found in other versions of the loathly lady story. Gower himself names a Florent along with Lancelot, Tristram, Generides, Partonope as one who 'sa Loialte guardoit' (Balade, xliii, st. 3: *French Works*, p. 366): a phrase certainly applicable to the hero of the present tale. He perhaps borrowed the name from the French romance *Octavian*: v. *Dict. des lettres français* (1964); a St. Florent appears in French hagiography.

1414–16. Gower constantly associates knighthood and 'worthy fame' (cf. e.g. iv. 1929–34), whereas in Chaucer's tale the 'lusty bacheler' seems at first regardless of both.

1424. A characteristic meiosis: cf. 1689 and 1766.

1427. *his oghne hondes*: instrumental in function (cf. *CT*, A. 3624) but perhaps historically an accusative: see G. V. Smithers (ed.) *Kyng Alysaunder* (EETS, 1957), l. 5885 n.

1428. *Branchus*: a name possibly of Gower's own choosing. In the French fourteenth-century Romance of *Perceforest* Branchus is a king of England.

1434–5. A typical dislocation: 'but that they bore in mind his knightly prowess'. Cf. 1722.

1485. *hath undertake*: The Fr. *passé indéfini* form generally represents a simple past tense in Gower: cf. e.g. viii. 2524, 2622 (VIII below).

1496. Cf. 'Weddynge of Sir Gawen' 1204: 'some sayd one, some sayd other'.

1497–8. 'according as Nature has arranged the blend of humours that produces one's temperament'.

1506. 'neither by astrological nor physiological inquiry' (unless *kinde* here = 'natural magic').

1509. 'and is destined utterly to be lost'. For *schape*, cf. 1544. Macaulay's 'prepared for the loss' seems unwarranted.

1518. *a* is emphatic: *one* point (*or* clause) of the oath made to the lady.

1533. *bihield hir redely*: 'glanced at her hurriedly'.

1541. Cf. *CT*, C. 213 ('Virginia, by thy name'), and B. 3982.

1566. *of park, of plowh*: an inclusive formula covering both enclosed land and arable.

1605. *thanne is ther no more*: 'the difficulty is disposed of' (?).

1610–11. Cf. 'Weddynge of Sir Gawen', 425: 'For where we haue sovereynte alle is ourys'.

1634. *mone*: OED defines as 'an old woman, crone' [a? ON *móna*, 'mammy'], but gives only this example. A metaphorical use of 'moon' (with reference to the yellowish look of a waning moon) seems equally likely: cf. Ruodlieb, xiv. 3–4 (see 1675 n.): *Femina, quae lunae par est in flore iuventae/Par vetulae simiae fit post aetate senectae.*

1643. *for yifte or for beheste*: 'by making any gift or'.

1651. 'That he will be in no position to boast'—'will be in, desperate plight'.

1662. Macaulay notes the verbal parallel in the 'Weddynge of Sir Gawen' at the same point in the story, where Sir Gromer says: 'I pray to God, I maye se her bren on fyre' (l. 475); and cf. the 'Marriage', l. 105: 'in a fyer I will her burne'.

1669. 'Instead of suffering his punishment' (?).

1675 ff. A restrained and effective variation on the traditional theme (found, e.g. in *Perceval*, 4611–37, and in the eleventh-century Latin epic *Ruodlieb*, xiv. 3–34) of female ugliness: cf. the depiction of Jealousy as a 'rympled vekke', *Romaunt of the Rose*, 4495–6, and of the 'auncian' in *Sir Gawain and the Green Knight*, 948 ff. The 'Weddynge of Sir Gawen' accentuates the grotesquerie by giving the 'vekke' teeth like boars' tusks and a ravenous maw. For later variations, see Wickert, *Studien*, p. 196.

1703. *Loke how*: 'just as'. The construction is related to the use of *loke who* (OE *lōca hwā*), 'whoever': see A. A. Prins, *English Studies*, xliii (1962), 165–9.

1708. Cf. v. 2833: 'Whan venym melleth with the sucre.'

1714. Cf. iii. 351–2: 'For it is seid thus overal / That nedes mot that nede shal'. In fact the proverb is not found elsewhere in this form; but 'he mot nedys go that the devyll dryves' (in Lydgate, Skelton, etc.) preserves its syntax and some of its meaning.

1723. *in ragges*: probably an ancient detail (not in Chaucer). In Torfaeus' rendering of Hrolf Kraki's saga the woman is *veste squalore obsita* (cit. Scott, *Minstrelsy of the Scottish Border*, 4th ed. iii. 65).

1727. Cf. *CT*, D. 1081: 'And al day after hidde hym as an owle'; the only point of close verbal likeness between Gower's tale and Chaucer's.

1786. Apparently a magical light which, penetrating the silk ('sendal') bed curtains, would make Florent's plight seem the harder, but would also enhance his final reward. In Chaucer the hag avers that she will be '*tomorne* as fair to seene / As any lady' (1245–6) though in fact the change is described as if it were immediate. Torfaeus, loc. cit., alters his source, omitting any mention of a lamp, and describes Helgi as noticing the change *prima luce*.

1819. A pleasing trait; but the sequel shows that she has her own reasons for concern.

1846. Cf. 'Weddynge', 752–3: 'And what the cause she forshapen was / Sir Gawen told the kyng'. The 'Marriage' uses the term 'witched'; cf. Gower's marginal gloss: . . . *ex eius Novercae incantacionibus* . . . *transformata* . . . (Macaulay, p. 74).

III

The tale of Canace (iii. 143–356)

The confessor tells this tale as a warning against Melancholy, which he has described as the first of the five servants of Wrath and which 'groweth of the fantasie Of love' (iii. 125–6).

Gower's source is Ovid, *Heroides* xi, which he has judiciously adapted and improved. Ovid gives the tale in the form of Canace's farewell letter to Macareus (see 269–70), in which she recalls their history before killing herself; it is only in presenting this letter that Gower follows Ovid at all closely.

In *CA*, viii, the confessor notes that in primeval times incestuous marriage was necessary for the propagation of the race; but he condemns its practice by Caligula, Amon, Lot, and Antiochus. In all those instances, however, he speaks only of immoderate lust overpowering passive victims; whereas in the present tale he emphasizes the strength of mutual passion and the impulses of nature, and depicts brother and sister as hardly responsible for their actions (see 178), reserving his strictures for the cruel father.

In *CT*, B. 57 ff., the Man of Law refers to the various stories that Chaucer had taken from Ovid 'in youthe' (the list in fact resembles a tally of Gower's classical love stories far more than a catalogue of Chaucer's extant stories in this vein) and then adds:

> But certeinly no word ne writeth he
> Of thilke wikke ensample of Canacee,
> That loved hir owene brother synfully;
> (Of swiche cursed stories I sey fy!)
> Or ellis of Tyro Apollonius
> How that the cursed kyng Antiochus

Byrafte his doghter of hir maydenhede,
That is so horrible a tale for to rede,
Whan he hir threw upon the pavement. (77–85)

That Chaucer knew of these stories independently of Gower is in any case likely and is suggested by (i) his form 'Apollonius' in contrast to Gower's 'Apollinus' in both text and margin and (ii) the detail of l. 85 above, of which Gower makes no mention. It remains probable that Chaucer was here covertly twitting his friend for using such shocking stories; but the general tone of the Man of Law's Prologue, with its allusion to Chaucer as 'lewed' (unlearned or unskilful in poetry, 47–48), and the Man of Law's own character as there indicated forbid us to describe the passage as a serious criticism of the friend whom he elsewhere describes as 'moral'.

160. *client*. Gower is the first to use this word in the transferred sense of (love) vassal.

169 ff. There is no allusion to Cupid in Ovid, nor, of course, to Natura or 'positive law'. For Gower's conception of the laws of Nature, see Bennett, *Parlement of Foules*, p. 197, n. 3. He refers to *lawe positif* (*lex positiva*, i.e. that determined by human authority) more disparagingly in *CA* Prol. 247; cf. *CT*, A. 1167 (in a similar context to the present).

174. *at large*: without regard to particular cases; 'so careless of the single life', as Tennyson was to put it. [on *and*, 171, see V. 2952 n.]

187–8: i.e. they had the misfortune to forget the use of their reason. Gower regularly depicts passion as overpowering reason, with baleful effects.

205. A recurrent *sententia*: cf., e.g. *CA*, v. 5123–4.

219. 'the child that had been born not long before'.

276. 'she could obtain by no means whatever'.

292 ff. Gower alters the sequence of events. In Ovid Canace knows before she writes the letter that her child has been exposed and believes that he has been torn to pieces by wild beasts.

298. Cf. viii. 2212 (VIII below).

299. *cares colde*: 'in desperate trouble *or* grief'. For other examples of the phrase (which is frequent in Chaucer), see *OED*, s.v. *cold*, a 9.

315. *basketh* (v. l. *baskleth*) in the sense 'wallows in blood' occurs only here, in Lydgate, *Troy Book*, v. 2505, and Skelton. The etymology is unknown: see H. Whitehall, *Philological Quarterly*, xiv (1935), 229.

330. *singe or rede*: probably a conventional phrase (= 'in any story') referring to public recitation: cf. *Troilus and Criseyde*, v. 1797 and Root's note.

331: 'Of such a thing done as that was'.

IV

Idleness in love; the tale of Rosiphelee: love and arms

(iv. 1083–1501; 1615–1770)

A close analogue to the tale of Rosiphelee, here told as a warning against the species of *Accidie* that is called Idleness, is found in the *De Amore* of Andreas Capellanus, a late twelfth-century treatise that includes a series of dialogues showing how love may be won.[1] At the beginning of the fifth dialogue (between a nobleman and a noblewoman) the man speaks, like Gower's Amans, of his continual preoccupation with his mistress: to serve and please her would be 'glorious beyond all else'. The woman in reply uses (also like Amans) the images of Love's court (*amoris curia*) and the service of Venus (*Veneris servitus*); and the nobleman then tells the following tale:

Whilst I was squire to 'the most noble lord Robert', riding through the royal forest of France one hot summer day I got lost, and whilst looking for my way I saw a large mounted company with one man riding in front on a very beautiful horse and wearing a golden diadem; he was followed by a fair company of women (*ingens mulierum chorus atque venustus quarum quaelibet in equo pinguissimo et formoso et suavissime ambulante sedebat*) [cf. 1309–11]. Each of the women was dressed in costly many-coloured garments and a cloak embroidered in gold, and was attended by three knights; a second group was surrounded by men troublesomely eager to serve them; and a third consisted of fair women in filthy clothes—garments of foxskin quite unsuited to the summer day; they rode stumblingly (*indecentes indecenter*) on lean halt horses without saddle or bridle (*et claudicantibus pedibus incedentes*) [cf. 1346 f.] and covered with dust. Far behind all these came a charming and dignified lady, also on a lean and dirty horse, who explained that this was the army of the dead and its commander the God of love who comes every week to give all their deserts. The first group knew whilst alive how to conduct themselves towards love's soldiers and favour sincere lovers; the second are those who served lust; the third (to which she belongs) closed the palace of love to all: hence they are punished—in ways that she reveals by taking the teller to the god of love, who enjoins him to warn those worthy folk who refuse to submit to love of the torments in store for them. The nobleman (like Rosiphelee) takes the story to heart.

The same story is found in *Le Lai du Trot*, of about the same date: see Trojel, ed. cit., p. xiv, n. 4; E. M. Grimes, *Romantic Review*, xxvi (1935), 313–21, and W. A. Neilson, *Romania*, xxix (1900), 86. At some points it resembles a tale reported about the same time by Walter Map

[1] Ed. E. Trojel, Copenhagen (1892): repr. 1964; trans. J. J. Parry, *The Art of Courtly Love*, New York (1941).

in *De Nugis Curialium*, Dist. ii. c. xii (trans. M. R. James, 1923): Edric the savage, Lord of Ledbury North, lost while hunting, sees a great dance of noble ladies 'most comely to look upon, finely clad in linen, greater and taller than our women, with one of them desirable beyond any favourite of a king', he falls in love, and with some difficulty he bears her off. For three days and nights he used her as he would. On the fourth day she addressed him as 'my dearest' promising him prosperity until he should reproach her about her 'sisters' or her origins. He married her, and lived happily (*temp*. William I) till he let fall an allusion to her sisters, whereupon she vanished for ever. This story recalls the Breton analogues to *Sir Orfeo* cited by A. J. Bliss in his edition of that poem, pp. xxxii–xxxiii; see 1312 n. below.[1]

The symbolic role of the halters was perhaps suggested to Gower by Andreas's description of the third knight accompanying each woman in the first company: *semper frenum tenebat in manu ut sine laesionis* [bridle] *offendiculo suavius equitaret in equo*; such details often persist in stories of this sort whilst larger elements undergo change. But certain details in Gower (the spring setting, the white horses) may derive from the *lai*, and others (e.g. 1348) may be his own additions, made simply to sharpen the picture.

1086 f. Cf. *CT*, G. 1–7 (second Nun's Prologue): 'The ministre and the norice unto vices / Which that men clepe in Englyssh ydelnesse . . .' etc., and Parson's Tale, 714 ('Idelnesse that is the yate of alle harmes'). This *topos* owed its popularity to the wide circulation of the *Disticha Catonis* and its use as a reader: Dist. 1, 2 runs:

> Plus vigila semper ne sompno deditus esto;
> Nam diuturna quies vitiis alimenta ministrat.

For collections of other instances, see R. Hazelton, *Speculum*, xxxv (1960), 365, n. 26, and cf. E. R. Curtius, *European Literature in the Latin Middle Ages*, pp. 88–89. *Sompno* in the distich is often glossed as *segnicies* and *alimenta* as *nutrimenta* (*angl.* 'noryshing').

Gower uses the *topos* again at iv. 3380, vii. 4384; and *Mirour*, 5266.

1096–7. *who as evere take* . . .: 'whatsoever man takes . . .'. For the sjv. cf. *CA*, iii. 2508, 'For what man the Croniques rede', and exx. collected by Macaulay, Prologue, 460 n.

1109. *cattus amat piscem sed non vult tingere plantas* [vel *plantam*, *lympham*] is a Med. Lat. proverb that was early taken into English: see *Oxford Dictionary of English Proverbs*, 2nd ed. p. 84. Gower gives another version

---

[1] The motif of a company of women riding magnificently arrayed by a forest-side occurs also in *Völsunga Saga*, c. 9.

of it in *Mirour*, 5395–8. Chaucer cites it in *House of Fame*, 1783–5 and it is the 'adage' referred to in *Macbeth*, I. vii. 44.

1104. *I yive a yift*: 'I warrant you'. Cf. *Handlyng Synne*, 3683, where it renders 'ne deuez duter'.

1125. For the tone and attitude of these lines, cf. *Roman de la Rose*, 2551–716 (where Amor describes how the lover thinks and behaves).

1149. 'Danger' elsewhere in *CA* is frequently personified, as in *Roman de la Rose* and hence in love-poetry generally; e.g. in *CA*, iii. 1537–83, where Daunger 'is mi ladi consailer', ever ready to prevent him from pleading his suit; i.e. it represents her prudence or standoffishness: cf. v. 6614–50. So a similar allegorical use is likely in the present line. For other examples, with comment, see Macaulay's note to i. 2443 and C. S. Lewis, *The Allegory of Love*, p. 124 and App. II, and W. R. J. Barron, 'Luf-daungere', in *Medieval Miscellany* presented to Eugène Vinaver (Manchester), 1965. Gower uses the word in a broader sense in *Mirour*, 2305 (see Macaulay's note thereto). See also viii. 2039 (VIII below).

1152. For the social aspects of chapel services and the opportunities for dalliance that they offered, cf. v. 7035–179 (a striking passage) and *Sir Gawain and the Green Knight*, 930 ff. (Gawain's first meeting with the lady of the castle). In the Provençal *Flamenca* the lover disguises himself as a 'clerk' in order to signal to his mistress at Mass.

1154. *lete ne mai*: 'I cannot neglect, leave off (doing)'.

1168. *ned hath no lawe*: an ancient legal maxim: *Necessitas non habet legem*: cf. *Piers Plowman*, B. xx. 10, and Skelton, *Colin Clout*, 864, etc.

1174. For weaving or embroidery as occupations of women of the upper classes, cf. *Piers Plowman*, B. vi. 10 f.

1180. 'mi contienance I pike': 'I cast a meaningful glance'. Cf. *CA*, i. 698:

> With yhe upcast on hire he siketh
> And many a contienance he piketh,
> to bringen hire in to believe
> Of thing which that he wolde achieve.

The phrase appears to be found only in Gower.

1189. She is the kind of fine lady whom Chaucer's Prioress was aping: cf. *CT*, A. 146. Hence the presence of dogs at the foot of effigies: e.g. the brass to Alice, wife of Sir John Cassy, at Deerhurst, Gloucs. (where the dog wears a belled collar and is named 'Terei').

1259. *the scole of love*: the discipline of love. In Thomas Usk's *Testament of Love* (*c.* 1384–7). Love, speaking of her 'trewe servaunt' Chaucer,

says 'his pere in scole of my rules coude I never fynde' (III. iv, l. 252). Cf. Gower's other figurative use, 'the scole of helle' (i. 436).

1274. For Cupid in this role cf. *Roman de la Rose*, 868 f. (= Romaunt, 880–3:

> But he can cherles daunten, he,
> And maken folkis pride fallen;
> And he can wel these lordis thrallen;)

see also *Parlement of Foules*, st. 2.

1304. Cf. viii. 837 (the King's daughter falls in love with Apollonius):

> . . . love hath mad him a querele
> Ayein hire youthe freissh and frele,
> That malgre wher sche wole or noght,
> Sche mot with al hire hertes thoght
> To love and to his lawe obeie.

1311. *on side*: 'side-saddle': like Chaucer's elegant Prioress in the Ellesmere drawings—not like the Wife of Bath.

1312. 'No earthly thing or person can compare with them for the other-worldly beauty in their faces.' The couplet has been justly praised, its meaning not always grasped. Some MSS. of the first recension have:

> The beaute of hire face schon
> Wel bryhtere þan þe Cristall ston;

whilst the second recension reads:

> The beaute of here fay(r)e face
> Ther may non erþly þing deface

with *faie*, cf. Marie de France's *Guigemar*: 'Dedenz unt la dame trouvee / Ke de beuté resemble fee' (703–4). It suggests that these creatures belong to or have come back from the world of 'faerie', or the dead: cf. *CT*, F. 96 (Sir Gawain, 'comen ayeyn out of Fairye'). In *Sir Orfeo*, 143 ff., a hundred knights and damsels appear on rich snow-white steeds, dressed in white, and commanded by a king wearing a crown made of a single precious stone that shone like the sun; Orfeo later (303 ff.) sees sixty ladies riding on palfreys 'gentil and iolif as brid on ris'. In that poem too the ladies are powerless to stay (cf. 1382 and 1346 with *Sir Orfeo*, 191 f., and 330: 'Sche most wiþ him no leng abide'). For white steeds associated with 'faery', cf. Child, *Ballads*, i. 286.

1451 ff. 'Among people of noble birth love is considered a service which every heart of sound feeling should undertake, to keep its desires on the true path'; 'every gentil herte' (cf. Guinizelli's 'cor gentil', Dante's 'gentil ratto' (*Inf.* v. 100) and the exx. in Chaucer collected in the *Knight's Tale*, ed. Bennett, l. 903 n.) will cover both sexes (cf. pl. *hise* 1453). But the exact force of 1451 is hard to render: the line appears to cover those who are of noble birth and consider themselves 'gentle'. The marginal gloss in some MSS.—*Non quia sic se habet veritas, set opinio Amantum*—suggests that the priest himself (or the scribe?) does not unreservedly endorse this doctrine—just as he does not commend love 'paramours' (see 1470 ff.). In discoursing on Chastity (vii. 4214) the priest begins by stating that 'the Madle is mad for the femele', but emphasizes by numerous *exempla* that desire must be ruled by the law of marriage—a point he makes also at 1476 f. In making it he steps beyond the demesne of Venus.

1483. *feste.* For a similar figurative use, cf. *TC*, iii. 1228.

1488 ff. 'So a maid should take warning by this as regards grudging her love, and should be slow in changing her mind when her youthful desires incline to marriage.' 'strange' is a favourite verb of Gower's, with various meanings, but the sense 'to grudge, be sparing of' is not otherwise evidenced before 1439. For 'lustes greene' (1491) cf. iv. 2309–10 ('For love hath evere hise lustes grene In gentil folk, as it is sene'), and Bartholomaeus *de proprietatibus rerum*, trans. Trevisa: 'A maide hatte virgo, and haþ þat name of grene [L. *viridior*] age' (cit. *MED*).

1455. The unexpected allusion to 'the knyht' may be a reminiscence of the knights who figure in the first company in Andreas's story summarized above.

1463. 'To consider (observe) the chief lesson.'

1489–90. 'as regards grudging her love and being slow in turning her youthful inclinations to marriage'.

1496. At v. 6418 ff., when Genius has praised the chastity of Valentinian, Amans uses this same argument against him.

[To the tale of Rosiphelee Genius adds the tale of Jephthah's daughter. Then, in response to a question from Amans, he indicates that Idleness has its contrary; witness those men who 'here loves boghte / Thurgh gret travail in strange londes'.]

1618–19. 'Meritorious achievement is so effective that in many places love is achieved the sooner' (because of it).

1625 ff. Cf. the list of crusading campaigns in which Chaucer's Knight took part (*CT*, A. 51 ff.). The 'grete see' is the eastern Mediterranean, the scene of some of that knight's exploits. 'Prus' suggests service with the knights of the Teutonic Order, who were active during the second part of the fourteenth century in subjugating the heathen Prussians and kindred and coterminous tribes. Henry Bolingbroke, the future Henry IV, whom Gower addresses in some copies of *CA*, took part in these Prussian wars in 1390–1. Rhodes (1630) had been in the possession of the Knights Hospitallers from 1309.

The career of one of Bolingbroke's retainers, Henry Lord Fitzhugh, born 1352, 'tres grand seignior et tres brillant et tres noble chevalier', provides an example of a knight who undertook most of the enterprises the confessor refers to: he fought against the Saracens, built a castle in Rhodes, and as late as 1408 fought in E. Prussia against the Letts.

1631. *Tartarie*. Tartar dominion at this date reached further west than the Persian Gulf. Tartary is mentioned in similar contexts in poems by Machaut and Deschamps (cit. Flugel, *Anglia*, xxix (1901), 440). 'Sarray, in the land of Tartarye' (*CT*, F. (9) = Tzarev (near Leningrad), a Tartar capital in Chaucer's time.

1632 ff. Cf. *Mirour*, 1261–6, where such behaviour is associated with 'la veine gloire'. The English passage is found separately in a Cambridge MS., which led the editor of *Cambridge Middle English Lyrics* to print it as a 'unique anonymous poem' (p. 38).

1649–50. A mixed construction, wavering between 'as me thenketh' and 'methenketh'.

1658. *Kaire*: the chief centre of Moslem power; at 2558 it appears to be thought of as the capital of Persia.

1664. Criticism of the knight errant who fights 'Devers Espruce et Tartary', 'pour loos' or 'pour m'amye', is found in *Mirour*, 23893 ff.; and Amans' attitude has its counterpart in that of Chaucer's Blanche who would 'holde no wight in honde . . .

> Ne sende men into Wallakye,
> To Pruyse, and into Tartarye,
> To Alysaundre, ne into Turkye,
> And byd him faste anoon that he
> Goo hoodles to the Drye Se
> And come hom by the Carrenar;
> And seye "Sir, be now ryght war
> That I may of yow here seyn
> Worshyp, or that ye come ageyn".
> She ne used no suche knakkes smale.'

Book of the Duchess, 1024–33; see Robinson's note.

The traditional view as expressed by Genius reappears in *Le petit Jehn de Saintré*, c. 6, though with interesting reservations.

1666 f. 'But let those cross the ocean whom Christ commanded to preach and teach his gospel to all creatures'—i.e. ecclesiastics and religious.

1679–80. Gower's attitude in the later *Peace* is somewhat different:

> And if men scholde algate waxe wrothe
> The Saracens, which unto Crist be lothe,

Let men ben armed ayein *hem* to fighte;
so mai the knyht his dedes of armes righte. . . .

(249–52)

But even there he is treating such warfare as 'blood-letting' in the body-politic rather than urging men to take the cross. The obligations of knighthood are discussed more fully in *VC*, v. cc. v–viii.

1684. '*I make a yifte*': 'I pledge myself.'

1691. 'Love will have his hour at last' (Dryden).

1693. Again Gower draws his instance from Benoit's *Roman de Troie* (18385 ff.) Cf. Lydgate, *Troy Book*, IV. 596 ff. . . . and Froissart, *Le Joli Buisson de Jonece*, 625–714.

1723. *fore*: Macaulay notes the unusual emphasis here thrown on the preposition in rhyme, and the resultant accompanying modification of form (usually fore). Cf. ii. 565–6 ('inne', rhyming with 'beginne').

1741. 'On what course I shall tack'. For the nautical phrase *OED* compares Fr. 'virer de bord', 'to turn the ship's side in another direction', and 'courir des bords', 'to tack'. In *OED* the first ex. (which also happens to be figurative) is from Bellenden's *Livy* (1533). See also p. xiv, n. 1.

1763–4. 'For the effect of everything reported must depend on the character of the result'(?)

V

The lover's wakefulness; the tale of Ceyx and Alcione;
the prayer of Cephalus (iv. 2771–3258)

[The confessor having warned against Somnolence, 'chamberlein' of Accidie, Amans is avowing his freedom from this vice.]

2778. The kind of dance that gave opportunity for love-making is described in the *Romaunt of the Rose* (783–91) and *CT*, F. 277 f. For late-night dancing with 'dere caroles' see *Sir Gawain and the Green Knight*, 1025–6.

2792. *to caste chaunce*: to tell the fortunes of lovers from the throw of the dice.

2793. 'or pose some *question d'amour*'—such as that asked by the Knight, *CT*, A. 1347 (see Robinson's note). A thirteenth-century French example is given by Huizinga, *The Waning of the Middle Ages* (1927), p. 71.

2794. The phrasing suggests that (as in *Troilus* itself: ii. 83) the reading may have been done by a third party.

2818. *noght on me along*: 'not on my own account, not my fault'.

2855. *whi ne were it . . .*: 'would it were'.

2894–5. i.e. he does not dream about material wealth as a wool merchant would do.

2913. *be my wille*: 'if I could have had my wish'.

2924. For the momentary disregard of the circumstances of the narrative, cf. *CT*, A. 1201 and *CA* viii. 2019 (VIII below).

2927. *Poesie*: Ovid, *Metamorphoses*, **xi.** 410–748. Gower keeps much less strictly to the sequence of events in Ovid than Chaucer had done in the *Book of the Duchess*, 62–220. He heightens suspense by omitting entirely the account of the storm in which Ceyx is drowned (*Met.* 480–569—a passage he had previously drawn on at length in *Vox Clamantis*, i. 1653–94). The monologue and *ipsissima verba* of the prayer that Chaucer attributes to Alcione (*BD*, 91–121) have no equivalent in Ovid. Chaucer's professed concern being with the powers of Morpheus, he omitted the metamorphosis on which Gower characteristically dwells.

The influence of Gower's version can be detected in a translation by Caxton of Ovid's story from a French rendering: see *Ovyde His booke of Metamorphose Books*, X–XV . . . ed. Stephen Gaselee and H. F. B. Brett-Smith (1924), pp. 51–59, and *Modern Language Review*, xlv (1950), 215–16. Dryden's Fables (1700) provide a version of the Latin.

2927. The same line introduces a later tale from the *Metamorphoses* (*CA*, vi. 485).

2928. *Trocinie*: *Met.* xi. 269: *Trachinia tellus* (Trachis, in Thessaly); the detail belongs to Ovid's preceding tale of Peleus.

2929. *hadde... to his wif*. The idiom survives in the Authorized Version: 'we have Abraham to our father' (Matt. iii. 9). Cf. iv. 1387 (IV).

2932 ff. Ovid has described this transformation in the preceding story (xi. 266–409). Chaucer finds it necessary to explain the purpose of Ceyx's journey, which Gower, like the French *Ovide Moralisé*,[1] treats as a pilgrimage because Ovid (413) says it was to *Clarium deum*—the Delphic oracle. The conception of 'grace' (2942) is Gower's.

2949. *as he which* . . .: modelled on OF 'comme celui qui': the clause is equivalent to a participial phrase, 'determined to go'. In Ovid Alcione argues at length that the sea is perilous and that he could go by land. Gower ignores the unconscious irony of her *pariter super aequora lata feremur* (443), which anticipates their final state.

2952. Displacement of *and* (and *bot*) is characteristic of Gower (cf., e.g. 2958, 3005 and (V) iii. 171)—as is the similar displacement of *et* in his

[1] Gower does not elsewhere reveal any reliance on this poem though it may have served as a precedent for his remaniement. At v. 6810 the word is used, in the same rhyme, of Hercules' journey with Eole.

French verse—but is also found in *Kyng Alysaunder* (xiiic), 2226, etc., and occasionally in later verse, e.g. 'Syne he ȝeid furth, a preva place & spyit', Kennedy, *Passion of Christ*, 423. In Ovid Alcione does not specifically make the request referred to at 2952; Ceyx swears of his own accord.

2958. In Ovid Alcione weeps in bed after Ceyx has left, but not at this point.

2963. *Ther was no care forto seche*: 'no sorrow was to be sought for', i.e. 'was absent'; 'her grief could not have been greater'. In Ovid she has counted the days and offered incense to *ensure* Ceyx's safe return. Gower shows her anxiety as much keener.

2968. *hath bede* (cf. 2978) is equivalent to a Fr. *passé indéfini* and should be translated as a simple past tense.

2979. *Induitur velamina mille colorum / Iris, et arquato coelum curvamine signans* (Ovid, 589–90). Cf. Caxton, ed. cit., p. 55: 'Yris her trewe messagier ... dyde on his reyny cope And descended by the Firmament by his bowe whych was bende & diversly clolowred' (Caxton follows Chaucer in making Iris male). 'rayny' is Gower's addition. Chaucer omits the rainbow entirely.

2985. *Est prope Cimmerios longo spelunca recessu / Mons cavus, ignavi domus et penetralia Somni* (Ovid 592–3). In *BD* Chaucer does not locate the cave but in the *House of Fame* he places it and the stream of Lethe 'besyd a folk men clepeth Cymerie' (73).

Spenser adapts Ovid's description in *Faerie Queene*, I. i. 39–43.

3000–2. The description of the cave in general follows Ovid's closely though with some reordering, but these two lines are Gower's own, if possibly suggested by Ovid's *non moti flamine rami* (600). Raucous crows and magpies are appropriately associated with tall trees, in which alone they nest.

3006. *Ante fores antri foecunda papavera florent . . .* (Ovid 605).

3009–10. A not inadequate equivalent to Ovid's soothing hexameters: *. . . per quem cum murmure labens / Invitat somnos crepitantibus unda lapillis* (603–4). Cf. *BD*, 161–2, where the streams are pictured as falling from 'clyves' (rocks or cliffs) and so making 'a dedly slepynge soun'. *Ovide Moralisé* (ed. Boer), 3454–5 renders the Latin as 'Si fet les chaillous resoner / Pour apetit de son[ge] doner' (cf. 3014).

3016. *hebenus that slepi tree*: simply *ebeno sublimis in atra* (*v.l. antro*) in Ovid: see *MLR* xlv (1950), 215–16. Ebony might connote the darkness of night, and so sleep: Cf. Herbert's *Evensong*: 'Thus in thy ebony box / Thou dost enclose us' (20–21). [For H. Bradley's suggestion that Marlowe knew Gower's line see *MLR* xv (1920), 86.]

3020. *fethrebed* is suggested by Ovid's *plumeus* (611) (qualifying *torus*), if not by the lines in which Chaucer expands Ovid's description of the coverings (cf. *BD*, 250–5, with Ovid, 610–11) when he promises a 'fethrebed' to Morpheus if he will grant him sleep.

3029. In Chaucer Iris cries 'Awake' three times. Ovid does not represent her as speaking but does describe Somnus as *iterumque iterumque relabens* (619).

3044. *lif*: the living being. Cf. *Sir Orfeo* 'O lef liif' (102, Orpheus addressing Eurydice).

Ithecus: Icelos in Ovid; cf. the distortion of Panthasas (3049) from Ovid's Phantasos (642). In Ovid (cf. Chaucer) Morpheus alone is sent to reveal the manner of Ceyx's death; see following note.

3061 ff. In Ovid Ceyx himself describes the fatal storm (663–6) and bids his widow mourn for him, whereas Chaucer has him bid her cease from her sorrow and bury his body. Gower has a vivid account (more closely resembling Chaucer's in *BD*) of an ominous 'swevene' in vi. 1523 ff.

3074–6. Ovid gives 20 lines to Alcione's lamentation but does not represent her maids as attempting to interpret the dream favourably; a detail which (especially in view of Gower's comment at 3054–5) preserves the suspense.

3087. Evidently partly suggested by Ovid's earlier description of Alcione's action while she dreamt: . . . *movetque lacertos / Per somnum, corpusque petens* . . . (674–5). In Ovid she is changed into a bird as she leaps, and kisses the corpse with her bill: *dilectos artus amplexa recentibus alis*; only later do the gods transform Ceyx. Gower relates the incident again, more briefly in *CA*, viii. 2650–6 (VIII below); cf. p. 126.

3122–3. Ovid leaves this unstated. Caxton says: 'And they ben called Alchyones or sea mews'.

3164. i.e. 'when it is broad daylight'.

3176 ff. 'I am well pleased that thou hast avoided [the sin of] slothful sleep at night when thou art a follower of Love, and that thou hast done thy best to ensure that thy mistress have no cause to complain [on that score].' For the sentiment, cf. *CT*, A. 97–98, 1042; but it is tempting to read into the lines Gower's humour at its quietest.

3196. Gower appears to have developed the whole of this scene from the two lines in which Ovid appeals to Aurora to hold back the dawn:

> At si, quem mavis, Cephalum conplexa teneres,
> Clamares: 'lente currite, noctis equi' (*Amores*, i. 13, 39–40)

Ovid's lines are probably the source of other medieval aubades or laments of lovers parted at dawn, from the Provençal poets (who assign them variously to the man or the woman) to Donne; but see L. P. Wilkinson, *Ovid Recalled*, p. 388 n.

3210. Gower loves scenes of night 'steeped in silentness': cf. v. 3958 (VI below), i. 1167, iii. 1384, etc.

3222. The sun enters Capricorn (Saturn's night 'mansion') on 22 Dec.

3242. In *CA*, vii. 1060 ff. Cancer is described as 'the propre hous and hold / Which apparteineth to the mone'. Luna 'exalted' in Cancer is a favourable sign.

VI

Jason and Medea (v. 3247-4174)

The confessor tells this tale as an example of perjury in love, which he has earlier described as a 'branch' of Covoitise, or Avarice. But it is only at the end that we are reminded of this connexion. The different emphasis in Chaucer's much briefer version (*Legend of Good Women*, 1368-1679) is very marked. Chaucer begins with an imprecation on 'Thou rote of false lovers . . . *sly* devourere and confusion of gentil wemen' (his oaths merely conceal his lust: 1380, cf. 1586 ff.) and concludes with reproaches culled from Ovid. Thrice within 200 lines Chaucer refers to sources which he cannot be troubled to reproduce (1457, 1558, 1678): a clear sign that the story never engaged his interest as it did Gower's.

The confessor implies (3245) that he will take as his authority for the story of the fleece 'the bok of Troie'. Chaucer begins by referring us to 'Guido', viz. Guido delle Colonne, whose prose *Historia destructionis Troiae* (1287) takes the story up to the flight from Colchos (books i–iii). Guido's *Historia* was the basis of Lydgate's *Troy Book* (*c.* 1412); but Gower, here as elsewhere, prefers to follow Benoit de Ste. Maure's verse *Roman de Troie* (1160) which likewise opens with the tale of the fleece (ll. 715-2078).[1] Gower dispenses with most of Benoit's repetitious rhetoric and so reduces 1,360 lines to some 700, whilst adding vivid passages of his own imagining (e.g. 3632-62).

3248. The claim is Gower's. Benoit merely says that Peleus was 'riches, proz, sages, corteis'.

[1] The story had a persistent appeal to artists (including illuminators of the *Roman de la Rose*). It is the subject of seven tapestry designs by Jean Fr. de Troy (1679-1752). De Troy's oil painting of Jason swearing his oath to Medea is now in the F. F. Madan collection in the Ashmolean Museum, Oxford.

3261. 'mout amot gloire e largece' (Benoit).

3265. The description of Colchos as an island (cf. *Mirour*, 3725) is due to Guido's *colcos insula*.

3273. Neither Benoit nor Guido mentions the gods; but in Benoit Medea later says 'Li deu i ont lor guarde mis' (1349).

3279–81. 'But, unwilling to give up the idea of such an enterprise, and wishing to undertake whatever befits a knight. . . .'

3282–4. This is as near as Gower ever comes to Benoit's actual words:

> Grant cuer e grant volenté
> D'aler en estrange regné
> E de veeir les regions
> Dont a oï nomer les nons. (867–70).

3290. Chaucer (like Guido and Benoit) represents Peleus as promoting the enterprise out of envy ('de mal porpens', Benoit) in the hope that Jason would perish. But 3291 probably refers to Jason.

3297. Benoit (like Guido) does not specify the month, but gives seven lines to the coming of spring.

3299. *yare*: 'quickly responsive to the helm'. The first instance of this sense, which is barely recorded again before Shakespeare.

3302 ff. 'What befell' is told in the story of Hypsipyle (*LGW*, 1465 ff.), which already shows Jason in the role of a false and deceitful lover.

3306. Cf. Benoit: 'Qui de sa terre nos congiee' (1065).

3318. Gower's addition.

3327. In Benoit they *all* array themselves in fine clothes first (1141–6).

3331. 'et mout par lor fist bele chiere' (Benoit, 1204).

3368. 'he bade Medea be sent for'.

3372. *which was him nothing loth*: 'who was far from being ill disposed towards him'. Guido says: . . . *repente in concupiscentia eius exarsit et ferventis amoris in animo caecum concepit amorem*, etc. Benoit, who emphasizes Medea's sufferings in love, says that she 'mout le desire a mariage' (1290).

3388 ff. A not uncommon situation in romances: cf., e.g.,

> Amdui erent de amur espris.
> El ne l'osot areisuner,
> E il dute a li parler (*Eliduc*, 502–4)

3414. The conflict is between love and his solemn undertaking to achieve the fleece (3280, 3363). It thus has some bearing on his later behaviour to Medea.

3416. *tok himself seint John to borwe*: 'invoked S. John's protection in his enterprise'. 'S. John to borwe' (lit. 'as pledge') was a common phrase of leavetaking (e.g. *CT*, F. 596).

3440. *he besoughte hir grace*: 'he begged her to show favour to him . . .', i.e. he acts as a 'courtois' lover. So at 3454 he addressed her as his lady, or mistress.

3446. 'Unless he knew what I know'.

3454. Cf. Benoit: 'Ma dame sereiz e m'amie / De mei avreiz la seignorie' (1435–6). In Benoit Jason promises to take her away as his wife and only then does she bid him visit her at night.

3463. 'For because of the good will shown to him at the outset it seems to him that all other difficulties are conquered': Gower's own comment. In Prol. 87–88* he cites the proverb 'a good beginning makes a good ending'.

3467. *daies yhe*: a periphrasis for the sun (but more often *worldes ÿe* (vii. 806): cf. *mundanus oculus* in Martianus Capella) found also in Lydgate *Troy Book*, ii. 5593; and cf. *Troilus and Criseyde*, ii. 904.

3484 ff. The incident (described at length by Benoit and Guido) may be compared with that in Boccaccio's *Il Filocolo* (ii. 181), where the lovers exchange formal vows and rings before the image of Cupid in sign of 'indissoluble matrimonie': a passage that is thought to be the source of *Troilus and Criseyde*, iii. 1362–8, though Chaucer mentions no image and no oath.

3487–8. 'that—so help him God—if Medea were to give him assistance . . .'. Identical rhyme between forms of identical meaning is common in ME as in OF.

3495. There is no reference to a maid in Benoit or Guido. Her entrance here means that she is privy to the wedding, and can plausibly be brought in when Medea swoons (3646–7)—another incident added by Gower.

3500 ff. In Benoit Medea tells all this to Jason in an effort to deter him, before either has confessed love.

3504. Benoit says that this smaller island lay about a league and a half from Colchos itself: 'N'ert guaires granz, mais mont ert beaux' (1810).

3524. 'that being one of the conditions'.

3534. *dethes wounde*: 'deadly wound': cf. *Troilus and Cryseide*, iii. 1697, and the similar attributive use of *worldes*, 3642 below.

3538. Momentary representation of *oratio recta*.

3557–8. Evidently suggested by the passage in Benoit (1619–20) in which Medea, at an earlier stage of the story, puts a pelisse over her chemise before getting out of bed to produce the image of Jupiter.

3573. *hold*: 'let him hold'. Macaulay compares 'And who that happeth hir to finde / For charite *tak* in his miynde . . .' (viii. 1128).

3579–80. Benoit speaks first of 'une figure / Faite par art e par conjure' (1665–6) and later of a written formula that Jason is to repeat. In *CA*, *Prol.* 918, 'hevenly figure' refers to the sun and moon. Gower presumably has in mind a figure involving astrology.

3595. 'which she gave him as a present'.

3637. *al hir world*: 'her fortune' or 'future hopes'. Cf. note to i. 178 (I).

3642. Cf. *Book of the Duchess*, 1038–40, and *House of Fame*, 256–8. The whole parting scene is Gower's invention.

3654 ff. 'It shall not be due to any sloth of mine if I do not carry out completely your injunctions according to your wish.'

3662. *mai*: not strictly accurate as applied to a wedded Medea. In *Mirour*, 3727, Gower calls her 'la meschine', which could mean 'maid', 'girl', *or* 'young woman'; see Macaulay's note on that line, and *Tr* v.1720.

3669. *undren hih*: Benoit's 'haute tierce', 1774: 'past 9 a.m.': cf. *prime*, 'first division of the day' (6–9 a.m.) 3880.

3688. *tok ore in honde*: corresponding to Benoit's 'No't o sei autre marinier' (1851); *sore him longeth*, 'is impatient'.

3707. *scherded*: found only here in the required sense of 'scaled', which confirms Macaulay's conjecture that it echoes Benoit's 'Les escherdes herice e tremble' (1919).

3732. A terse visualization derived from Benoit's description of the fleece *before* Jason has achieved it (cf. also 3743):

> . . . le mouton, qui mout resplent:
> Grant clarté done l'or vermeil
> Contre la raie del soleil (1884–6).

3735 ff. Benoit represents Medea as watching Jason *depart* while she weeps 'en une tor', changes colour, and:

> Belement dist entre sez denz
> Jason, sire, beaus amis genz
> Mout sui por vos en grant error,
> Quar jo vos aim de grant amor', etc. (1861–4)

Benoit gives her no prayer corresponding to 3739–40.

3738. *nouther ten ne twelve*: an emphatic formula.

3747. 'If only he were ashore!'

3771. In Benoit the fleece also is regarded as a 'chose faee' (1994), and Jason's victory is ascribed to divine favour.

3776. In Benoit 'mout en a li reis grant *ire*'. In Guido Oetes receives Jason *fictitia jocunditate*, being envious.

3789–91. Guido says that she would have kissed him ardently *si licuisset*. Gower has in mind the custom in his own time, of both sexes kissing at meeting and parting: *mos nunquam satis laudatus* said Erasmus writing from England to Andrelinus (1499); cf. Cavendish, *Life of Wolsey, sub anno* 1527.

The following passage, concluding with a touch worthy of Chaucer in 3800, is Gower's addition.

3807. *tok a sopp*: 'made a slight repast'.

3812 ff. Benoit simply says that the Greeks remained for another month (as in Guido) and that finally Medea committed the 'grant folie' of running off with Jason, who 'puis la laissa, si fist grant honte' (2036).

3837. They eat in pairs, as customary in the fourteenth century. Cf. *Sir Gawain and the Green Knight*, 109 (and n. in EETS ed.), 1003–19.

3915. *caliphe*: apart from the phrase 'calypp ad carriand ligna' cit. *MED*, this is the only instance of the word (of Arabic origin?) in ME.

3927 ff. Neither Benoit nor Guido relates the remainder of the tale, for which Gower turned to Ovid, *Met.*, vii. 159–293. He again adds numerous touches of his own, e.g. 3967, 4036, 4172–4.

3984–5. Ovid has merely *quae coeptis conscia nostris / Adjutrixque venis cantusque artisque magorum* (194–5). [Edrates = Hecate.]

3994. Gower either misread *creteis regionibus* (223: 'chalky regions') himself or followed a MS. with the reading *Cretis*. Hence the geographical confusion in the following lines.

4006. *Eridian*: Eridanus? Ovid's *Apidanus* (228: a river in Thessaly).

4011. *Rede See*: Macaulay suggests that Gower read *rubrum mare* for Ovid's *refluum mare* (267).

4039. For Ovid's *verbenis silvaque incinxit agresti* (242): 'she wreathed them with boughs from the wild wood' [see Add. Notes, p. 176].

4045. *wether*: Ovid lists the parts of various animals, but does not mention a ram. For Gower's knowledge of sorcery see *CA*, vi. 1292–end.

4052–3. Ovid has merely *Umbrarum rogat rapta cum conjuge regem* (249).

4064–114. Many of the details are new, including 4064, –68, –73, –99 f., and the description of Medea as *faie*, 4105—as if to make her a fit mate for Jason (cf. 3769 above).

4127–9. *Nec defuit illis / Squamea Cinyphii tenuis membrana chelydri* (Ovid, 271–2), 'the scaly skins of small Cinyphean snakes'. Gower makes what he can out of two uncommon words.

4138. *seewolf*. In Ovid a werewolf: *ambigui prosecta lupi* (271). Gower probably had in mind the (fabulous) amphibious beast of prey referred to by 'Robert of Gloucester' and Topsell (see *OED*, s.v.[1]) rather than the fish described in *OED*, s.v.[2]

4156. *was of assay*: 'that was of proven worth'.

4170. Suggested by Ovid's: *et olim / Ante quater denos hunc se reminiscitur annos* (292–3).

VII

Tereus and Procne (v. 5551–6047)

This tale of warning against the sin of 'Ravine' or rape (a branch of Avarice) is freely adapted from Ovid, *Met*. vi. 424–674. Gower omits (*inter alia*) the long account of the way in which Tereus induces Pandion to allow Philomela to return with him (447–510) and Pandion's parting words to them (447–510), Philomela's rescue from imprisonment, and most of the shocking details of the death of Ibis and the feasting on his flesh. Ll. 5734–68, 5816–60, 5915–27, 5943–6029 represent Gower's own contributions, the last of these additions being, as Macaulay noted, especially characteristic. Chaucer's outline of the same story, or most of it, in *LGW*, 2228–93, in general follows Ovid. [See Add. Notes, p. 176.]

5555. *who so thenke therupon*: 'if you wish to know it'.

5564. *of his pourveance*: 'looking to the future'.

5565. Gower omits Ovid's reference to the ominous presence of the Eumenides, probably because it would require too much explanation.

5618. *assoteth*. Gower's favourite usual description of passion unrestrained by reason: cf. e.g. i. 781, 2596, ii. 2269, viii. 2036 (VIII below).

5624. In Ovid Tereus is inflamed as soon as he sees Philomela (on landing): [*non secus*] *quam si quis canit ignem supponat aristis / Aut frondem positasque cremet faenilibus herbas* (456–7). But Ovid makes it clear that the rape takes place after they had reached Thrace (where Tereus imprisons Philomela in a hut in the woods).

5634. Adapted from Ovid's description of Philomela's later state, when *Illa tremit, velut agna pavens* (527).

5644. A fusion of two similes referring to a bird of prey in Ovid (516–18, 529–30).

5670. *tellen tale and ende*: 'tell the tale from beginning to end'; originally 'on ende', as in 'setten spel on ende', *Dame Sirith*, 62; *Cursor Mundi*, 1295, etc.: see B. Miller, *Notes and Queries*, Oct. 1961. [See Add. Notes, p. 176.]

5671–4. ll. 5671–2 are Gower's addition, and 5673–4 strengthen the force of Ovid's *audiet haec aether et si deus ullus in illo est* (548) and so make the passage fully consistent with the prayer inserted later (5741).

5688. Gower's own wry comment.

5695. *the deth.* In ME *deth* is often preceded by the article, presumably in imitation of French usage.

5700. Gower's touch is more effective than Ovid's conceit about the severed tongue (556 f.).

5708. *that foule him falle*: 'to whom may evil befall'.

5718–19. 'and was almost at the point of death as a result of hearing this news': cf. i. 289–90: 'Between the lif and deth I herde / This prestes tale er I answerde',[1] and see viii. 2451 (VIII below).

5728–9. 'She found it would do no good to go on lamenting.'

5730. *guile under gore*: 'deceit concealed, as it were, under a cloak'. *under gore* is usually part of an alliterative phrase, referring primarily to a woman's skirt or gown, e.g. *goodlich under gore.*

5731–2. A typical transition formula in medieval romance. Cf., e.g. Malory, *Works* (ed. Vinaver, 1947), p. 1130, l. 4.

5779. In Ovid the messenger is a woman. Gower alters to accord with medieval custom.

5802. Ovid says that this was done by night during a festival of Bacchus, when the Thracian matrons had special licence.

5866–7. 'But anyone who had heard the two of them could never have ceased to lament over the grief that afflicted them both.'

5846. Apollo is not usually described as god of rest, though the attribute accords with his character as god of music. As the sun, he gives food to men (5855) inasmuch as he brings about the increase 'Of every plaunte, herbe, tree and flour' (*CT*, F. 1031–2; cf. Henryson, *Testament of Crisseid*, 198 ff.).

5877. A meiosis typical of Gower.

5890–4. The madness is Gower's gloss on the deed of horror.

5936 ff. Ovid does not mention the gods (to whom Gower throughout the tale gives a more active role). He says merely:

> Quarum petit altera silvas,
> Altera tecta subit. Neque adhuc de pectore caedis
> Excessere notae; signataque sanguine pluma est. (668–70)

5960 ff. Cf. the description of 'le temps joly / Du Maii, quant la deesce Nature / Bois, champs et prées de sa verdure / Reveste, et l'oisel font leur cry' in *Mirour*, 939 ff.; but there it is the time for the wedding of the seven sins: see p. 131 below.

[1] A confused echo of the idiom is in the *Court of Venus*, st. 6 (see p. 165).

5995. Cf. Latin headpiece, p. 1.

6011. *chitreth*. The verb is used to describe a swallow's twitter in *CT*, A. 3258 (*v.l.*), and *Troilus and Criseyde*, ii. 68 (in a stanza about Procne).

6044. Gower's improvement on Ovid's *cui stant in vertice cristae* (672).

6047. Cf. 'the false lapwynge, ful of trecherye', *Parlement of Foules*, 347.

VIII

The confessor's final counsel, absolution, and farewell to love
(viii. 2013–end)

2017. *ayein kinde*: as in incestuous love, the sin that in *CA* takes the place of *luxuria*. The confessor has just concluded the long story of Apollonius of Tyre, beginning with Antiochus' incest.

2019. *tofore rede*: see n. on iv. 2924 (V above).

2022. As the end of the shrift approaches (cf. 2059 ff.) the confessor emphasizes the themes of 'honest' love and reason, which have been threaded through the work: see Bennett, op. cit., p. xxii above.

2055–6. 'And the longer I try the less knowledge I have [i.e. the less I learn about love] yet still I cannot give it up.'

2072–4. Cf. *CT*, I. 47 ('To knytte up al this feeste, and make an ende').

2077. *toward*: 'in attendance on': cf. *OED*, *toward*, prep. 2† *b*.

2101. Evidently proverbial; not found elsewhere [*aisshe*, collective sing.: 'ashes'].

2111–12. 'every man has a kingdom that it is his responsibility to rule over—namely himself'. The sentiment is as old as Epictetus ('No one is free who commands not himself': *Encheiridion*, c. 110) and recurs in Macrobius (*Comment*. I. viii. 51). Gower's phrasing of it is reminiscent of Dante, *Purg.* xxvii. 142 (. . . 'io te sopra te corono e mitrio'). Cf. also *Ayenbite of Inwyt* (EETS OS 23), p. 85, where it is attributed to Seneca.

2116. Cf. ii. 2494–5: 'The schip of love hath lost his rother / So that he can no reson stiere.'

2160–1. 'the hart that goes at liberty in the glade has no inkling of what troubles an ox'.

2166–7. 'he would certainly behave just as the other man does, and perhaps worse, in his own way'.

2197 ff. 'There was never yet a man who could pay any regard to reason when love was refused him.' Cf. Dunbar: 'Discretioun and Conscideraunce / Ar both out of hir [sc. Love's] governaunce.'

2210. Cf. i. 113 (I above). The whole confession has been heard *en plein air*.

2212. Cf. iii. 298 (V above) and *VC*, ii. I, 1 : *Incausti specie lacrimas dabo, de quibus ipse / Scribam.*

2216. A lover complains to the god of love in *La Panthère d'Amours*, an early verse–offshoot of the *Roman de la Rose*. For the device in general see Chaucer's 'Complaints' *to Pity* (with its 'bill' 44), *to his Lady*, etc., the first named (like parts of the others) being in the same 'rime royal' (OF 'chant royal') metre as Gower's, and perhaps the earliest English example of this verse-form, which Gower may therefore owe to Chaucer; it appears chiefly in formal or serious poems or passages. Gower's skill in this kind of poetry is sufficiently evidenced in his French balades to make it unnecessary to suppose that this Complaint had a French original. The genre doubtless owed something to classical exemplars, e.g. the end of Œnone's letter to Paris in Ovid, *Heroides*, v. 149–58, which Gower knew and which Pandarus cites (*TC*, i. 659–65).

It was probably Gower's use of the device that led to its appearance in Lydgate's *Temple of Glass* (143–246) and the *Parlement of Love*. The fragmentary *Court of Venus* (*c.* 1560) follows Gower in having Genius present the bills to Venus: see E. K. Chambers, *Sir Thomas Wyatt*, p. 211.

2224. Complaint to Nature is at least as old as Ausonius (fourth century): *Conquerimur, Natura, brevis quod gratia florum est.*

2240. Pan is also described as the 'god of kinde' in *BD*, 512–13. The association of the pastoral god's name with πᾶs, πᾶν led to his being thought of as *totius naturae deus* (so Servius, *Commentary on Virgil*, Ecl., ii. 31; cf. Isidore, *Etym. Lib.* xi. 81–83); see further Bennett, *The Parlement of Foules*, p. 207. The reference in the following line is presumably to Pan's love for Syrinx as described in Ovid, *Met.* i. 699 ff.

2241. Cf. Pandarus's 'I hoppe alwey byhynde', *Tr*, ii. 1107.

2253. Cf. *CA*, vi. 330–50:

> For Jupiter aboven alle,
> Which is of goddes soverein,
> Hath in his celier, as men sein,
> Tuo tonnes fulle of love drinke,
> That maken many an herte sinke
> And many an herte also to flete,
> Or of the soure or of the swete
>
> . . . .
> Cupid is boteler of bothe
>
> . . . .
> Bot for so moche as he blind is
> Ful oftetime he goth amis . . .

—a passage probably modelled on *Roman de la Rose*, 6813–33, though there 'la taverniere' is Fortune. There is a brief allusion to the topic in Boethius, *De Cons. Phil.* II, pr. ii *ad fin* (see Chaucer's translation).

2259. Cf. Balade XX. st. 2 (*Works*, III. 354).

2266. See (e.g.) *Met.* i. 468 ff. where Cupid's golden darts are described; cf. Bennett, op. cit., p. 86, n. 2, and Boccaccio, *De Genealogia Deorum* . . . IX. iv. For Cupid's blindness see i. 45 n. (I above); *LGW*, F. 325 refers to his 'firy dartes' (and cf. e.g. Dunbar's *Golden Targe*, 111). [See also p. xiv, n. 1.]

2273–4. I cannot find a precise equivalent in Ovid.

2275 ff. Saturn is usually represented as unfavourable to lovers: cf. *CT*, A. 1328 and Henryson, *Testament of Crisseid*, 152 ff. Hence the conjunction ('conseil') of the two planets was inauspicious. But the reference may rather be to Saturn's traditional association with the sixth age of man—that of the 'lean and slippered pantaloon': cf. 2407 ff. and 2666 ff. below. 'Hevynesse' (2277) will allude to Saturn's association with pensive melancholy, and his metal is lead.

2315. It is usually Cupid who is depicted as standing near a tree: cf. *PF*, 211, and Panofsky, *Studies in Iconology*, fig. 75.

2312. *the montance of a mile*: 'the time taken to walk a mile'; cf. 'the mountaunce of a furlong wey of space' (*LGW*, F. 307).

2319. *halvinge a game*: 'half in jest'. Gower uses the adverb *halvinge* (< OE *healfunga*) frequently, but no later examples are recorded.

2328. 'But that must be settled between you and her.'

2341. Alanus de Insulis, *De Planctu Naturae*, is just such a complaint: for accounts of it, see F. J. E. Raby, *History of Christian Latin Poetry*, ii. 16 ff. or C. S. Lewis, *The Allegory of Love*, pp. 105–9. 'Nature se pleint' of Sodomy (as well as of homicide and ire) in *Mirour*, 9505–6 (and 4923, 5103).

2342 ff. This conception of a court of Venus with quasi-legal forms and powers was much favoured by fifteenth-century poets. Cf. *The Kingis Quair*, 632 ff., and exx. cited in *The Floure and the Leafe*, ed. D. Pearsall, p. 55. At ii. 39 ff. the other suitors ('lusti' and 'freisshe') of the lady have been described as 'the court of Cupide'.

2363–5. In parliamentary usage the formula 'le roi s'avisera' implied refusal of a petition ('bille'). Cupid is later to appear 'in parlement' and be 'avised' by Venus: 2454, 2785.

2367 f. 'Healing is not to be looked for in me by you and old lovesick folk like you. It is not merely a matter of luck, as you would have it, but depends on your acting as required by reason, which is consonant with / appropriate to / the nature of love'. 2369–70 have singular forms in the group of MSS. that omits 2371–6; they give the first clear indications that *Amans* is an old man. The Latin verses found in the full text (Macaulay, ii. 450) between 2376 and 2377 may be read as a complement to the doctrine in Chaucer's story of January and May (the Merchant's Tale).

2379. *rageman.* A game of chance in which the players evidently drew items (? verses) from a bundle or roll [*ragmanrole* > *rigmarole*, q.v. in *OED*] originally resembling a rolled-up document to which pendant seals were attached. The simile is especially appropriate as there is some evidence that love-fortunes were told by this means: see J. Stevens, *Music and Poetry in the Early Court*, p. 174. [*peis*, 2380 = weight.]

2403–4. Cf. Ovid: *Turpe senex miles, turpe senilis amor* (*Amores*, i. 9. 4).

2408. Chaucer applies the same phrase to himself in *Lenvoy a Scogan* ('Lo, olde Grisel lyst to ryme and playe')—a poem in which he suggests that he and Scogan are too old for Cupid's notice: cf. *LGW*, G, 262.

2415. *faile upon the fet* (= OF *fait*): 'be wanting when the time for action comes'. (but OF *sur le fait de* = 'on the subject of': cf. Caxton, 'upon the feat of').

2416. *beau retret*: 'a graceful withdrawal'. The phrase appears also in the *Assembly of the Gods* (questionably attributed to Lydgate), 1063.

2421. *tak hom . . .*: 'recall'; much the earliest figurative use of the phrase recorded.

2426. An allusion to a proverb recorded only by Ray (1678), in the form 'There belongs more than whistling to going to plough'.

2435. For the substantival use of verbs and phrases, cf. ii. 473 ('And is al war of hadde I wist') and vi. 923–4 ('But al of woldes and of wisshes Therof have I my fulle disshes') and 2435 below.

2454 ff. The company of lovers led by Cupid has antecedents in French and English love poetry, notably in the prologues to *LGW* (F. 210 ff.) and Froissart's *Paradys d'amours*, 930 ff. (cited in part by Macaulay) and *La Panthère d'Amours* (cf. *Venus la deesse d'amour*, st. 122). The *locus classicus* is *Roman de la Rose*, 727–903 (= Chaucer's *Romaunt*, 744–917). The rival companies of the flower and the leaf (first celebrated by Deschamps) referred to in *LGW*, Prol. F. 88, etc., were evidently a feature of court fashion in Richard II's reign. But it is not till the fifteenth century that they are described as representing the pleasure-loving (the flower) and the chaste and brave—including the Nine Worthies, laurel-crowned—(the leaf): see Pearsall's edition of *The Floure and the Leafe*, p. 22 f.; that poem likewise describes dancing to the sound of music as at 2477 ff. below. Dunbar's

Golden Targe represents a variant of the same theme, the company of Nature, Venus, Flora, etc., being followed by the court of King Cupid; but all are alike clothed in green (as in Froissart).

2462. *Jonece* figures in the garden of Deduit (mirth) in the *Roman de la Rose* (1281 in Chaucer's version), but as a girl less than twelve years old, accompanied by a 'vallez' ('bacheler'). In the *Paradys d'Amours* Jonece proposes that the company make green chaplets of flowers.

2469 f. For the attire cf. *Paradys d'Amours*:

> Les dames furent orfrisies
> Tout perlees et bien croisies
> Et li signeur avoint cor
> D'ivorie bendé de fine or.

The new guise of Beawme: After Richard's marriage to Anne of Bohemia in 1382 the decorative arts of Bohemia (then at their peak) had a marked influence in England. Queen Anne herself evidently set the style in women's fashions (and 2502 ff. make it clear that Youth's 'rout' includes women). The court dress of the period is illustrated in the miniature referred to above (p. vii, n. 2), which shows Chaucer in the presence of the queen and her court. In Bohemian painting of the time a richly ornamented gold circlet is a feature of female dress: in paintings of the Virgin it is shown worn forward on the brow, below a jewelled crown edged with large upstanding gold leaves; large square gold brooches also figure prominently—which is perhaps why Chaucer's fashionable Prioress wore a 'brooch of gold ful sheen' inscribed with the Queen's initial (*CT*, A. 160–1; cf. *Tr*, i. 171). The queen in *LGW* (who may represent Anne) wears a white crown 'with many floures . . . of o perle fyn, oriental' on a *fret* of gold; and the god of love, who accompanies her, wears 'a fret of rede rose leves' (*LGW*, F. 221 ff.). When Gower himself pictures Achilles, disguised as a woman, with 'frette of perle upon his hed' (v. 3015) he is evidently thinking of the fashion of his own time. Thus 'the new guise' may refer specifically to costly hair frets; the leaves and flowers in such a fret would evidently be artificial: cf. the citation in *OED*, s.v. *fret*, sb^1, s.a. 1418.

Similar attention to details of dress is found in *The Floure and the Leafe* and the *Assembly of Ladies*. For a description of one of Richard II's elaborate garments (including a doublet embroidered with gold orange trees and silvergilt oranges) see Joan Evans, *English Art 1307–1461*, p. 84.

2482 ff. All instruments notable—in contrast to those named at 2677 ff. —for their loud shrill notes: cf. *House of Fame*, 1217–19, 1239–40. (And cf. ib. 1235, *love-daunces, springes*, for *springe*, 'leap', 2487, where *freissh* = 'gaily'.)

2492–3. 'dismissing Sorrow, so that there was no room for him at all'.

2500 ff. With this roll-call of famous lovers, cf. *LGW*, G. 203–20, *PF*, 285–91 (discussed in Bennett, *The Parlement of Foules*, pp. 101–4), and *Paradys d'Amours*, 974 ff. None of the classical names occur in Froissart's list; on the other hand, he has several Arthurian names that are absent from Gower's. Since the stories of many of the lovers here named have been told in the *Confessio* (but not the tale of Polyxena and Pyrrhus, 2592, though they are mentioned in other contexts) the catalogue here has the special function of summarizing and recalling them.

2500. '. . . Tristram, who remained with the bele Yseult' [see p. 176 below]. Genius has referred to the story of the love-potion given by Brangwen as 'in every mannes mouth' (vi. 470 ff.). For versions of the story known in fourteenth-century England see R. S. Loomis (ed.), *Arthurian Literature in the Middle Ages* (1959), pp. 514 ff.

2502. Galahaut: Malory's 'Haut Prince', who in the French Prose Lancelot brings about the meeting between Lancelot and Guenevere and himself becomes the lover of the Dame de Malehaut whose advances Lancelot had scorned.

2508 f. Genius has told how Hercules forsook Deianira for Iole and as a result perished from the burning shirt of Nessus (cf. 2561) in *CA*, ii. 2262 ff. He derived the tale from *Met.*, ix. 101 ff. and *Heroides*, ix.

2513 ff. The story of Theseus' abandonment of Ariadne for Phaedra is told in *CA*, v. 5395 ff.; that of Telamon, and the rebuilding of Troy, at v. 7195 ff.

2531. Gower has altogether seven allusions to the story (including *CA*, ii. 2451, v. 7597, *Mirour*, 5251–4). Possibly he knew of other versions besides Chaucer's.

2544. Achilles is not usually characterized as lovelorn in medieval references: Chaucer saw him as cruel (*HF*, 1463). But Dares and Dictys and the romances deriving from them describe him as dying as a result of love for Polyxena: according to these versions of the Homeric story Achilles withdrew from fighting in order to end the war so that he might wed Polyxena; it is only to avenge his own men that he returns to the battlefield (and kills Troilus). Hecuba thereupon has him meet her in the temple of Apollo, supposedly to discuss his marriage, but in fact to allow Paris to kill him there: see M. Scherer, *The Legends of Troy in Art and Literature* (1963), pp. 101–2.

2554–8. The story of Phillis and Demephon is told at iv. 731 ff., of Theseus and Ariadne at v. 5231 ff.

2568. The story of Achilles' concealment among the daughters of

Lichomedes, his love for Deidamia, and his detection by Ulysses and Diomede, is told at v. 2961 ff. (based on Statius, *Achilleid*, i. 197 ff.): see Scherer, op. cit., pp. 42–43.

2572–3. Cf. *LGW*, 696 ff. Macaulay suggests that Chaucer derived the detail of the snakepit from the account of Cleopatra's death cited by Vincent of Beauvais in his *Speculum Historiale* from Hugh of Fleury: 'in mausoleum odoribus refertum iuxta suum se collocavit Antonium. Deinde admotis sibi serpentibus morte sopita est'; a description that might easily suggest a grave full of serpents.

2582. Thisbe makes no such reproach in the story as told at iii. 1376 ff.

2593. Guido delle Colonne states that Polyxena was killed by Pyrrhus in the temple of Apollo: cf. Boccaccio, *De claris mulieribus*, xxxi. Lefevre (*Recueil des Histoires de Troie*) states that he did this because she had caused the death of his father Achilles: see Scherer, op. cit., pp. 126–7.

2599. Circe and Calypso are mentioned in the account of Ulysses' wanderings at vi. 1427 ff. Their appearance in the present context is surprising, but sorts with Gower's view of love as often partly an enchantment.

2605. The presence of four faithful wives (their stories have been told at iv. 152 ff., vii. 754 ff., vii. 1920 ff., and iv. 2928 ff. respectively) is revealing: cf. p. xiv. (The pre-eminence Chaucer accords to Alceste in *LGW*, Prol. G. is probably out of compliment to Queen Anne.)

2646. Exclamatory, with aposiopesis of some such statement as 'tell me'.

2662. The household of Love in Froissart's *Trèsor Amoureux* has such personified offices, e.g. Hardement is constable, Desir and Penser are marshals (404 ff.). For later exx. see Pearsall, ed. cit., p. 56.

2633. *lay*: ? 'law' (OF *lei*). Perhaps of general import: 'so busy about his business'.

2667. *Elde*. Here masculine, and more dignified than his ugly and feeble feminine counterpart in *Roman de la Rose*, 339 (= *Romaunt*, 349 ff.).

2678–9. All the instruments here mentioned were of light, low tone.

2689 ff. A version of the traditional list of worthies overcome by love: cf. vi. 93–99, *Sir Gawain and the Green Knight*, 2417–20, and Douglas, *Eneados*, Prol. iv. 29 ff. Comparetti, *Virgilio nel Medio Ævo*, ii. 109 ff., gives further references. For the story of Aristotle's being ridden as a horse by Phyllis—frequently illustrated in the Middle Ages (e.g. in a mural at San Gimignano)—see G. F. Black's ed. of the *Sevin Seages* (STS, 1931), p. 395. For Virgil's love for an (unnamed) emperor's daughter, who left him suspended in a basket, see ibid., p. 399, Comparetti, op. cit., ii. 108 ff., 245–6, and J. W. Spargo, *Virgil the Necromancer* (1934), pp. 136–7.

2698 f. A legal figure referring to the securing of a person by the authority of a court (cf. *Piers Plowman*, A. ii. 212)—in this case the court of Venus.

2718. *Sortes*: A medieval form of Socrates, who plausibly figures in this list as the elderly husband of the shrewish Xantippe (cf. *Mirour*, 4166 ff.). Gower uses the correct form of his name elsewhere; it is not found in the lists of 'assoted' lovers cited by Comparetti.

2732. For the personification, cf. Chaucer's *Complaint unto Pity*.

2765. *for no ryote*: 'however unrestrained his manner of life' (?). Cf. v. 7130* f. (Lucius 'was not wys in his doinge. / But every riot atte laste / Mot nedes falle . . .').

2799. As described at the beginning of the poem: i. 144 ff. (I above).

2812. For the binding power of love cf. *TC*, iii. 1766 ff. (adapted from Boethius).

2815–16. For the rhyme, cf. *OED*, s.v. *key*, pronunciation note, and the exx. under (2). For the salve of 2817 cf. OF *Eneas* 7986.

2821. A mirror is one of Venus' regular attributes, but she is usually depicted beholding her own face.

2862. *Raison* has a similar function in the *Roman de la Rose* but is there personified as feminine.

2872. *what love was*: 'what sort of a power / person Love was'.

2897. In accord with the doctrine of religious confession. The penitent need not be further concerned about the sins confessed, and the priest, bound under the seal of secrecy, in fact does put them from his mind.

2904. *a peire of bedes*: a rosary (cf. *CT*, A. 159; the phrase may still be heard in Ireland and America), the gauds being the larger beads (often of gold) set at regular intervals among the smaller (usually of coral). Assuming that one letter of the inscription was set on each of the larger beads, there would be ten gauds.

The whole of this passage shows a sensitive adjustment of secular to spiritual values comparable in its minor way to that proposed by Dante in *Convivio*, iv. xxviii. A faint hint of *Amans*' age and lot in love has been given by the priest's comparison of his state to bare winter (v. 7824); and his 'lusti youthe' is referred to as past at vi. 1366.

2926. *as men telleth*: 'as one says', = 'as is said'; possibly alluding to Chaucer's description, see p. vii above.

2941–57. This part of the *Conclusio* is found in copies of the first recension only. The opening lines recall Chaucer's own account (in the mouth of the Man of Law) of his youthful works and his (later) stories of 'noble wyves and thise loveris' (*CT*, B¹. 59); cf. *HF*, 626 f. They are in marked contrast to Cupid's charge in the G recension of *LGW*, 257, that [Chaucer] 'makest wise folk fro me withdrawe'—an attitude that Cupid associates with signs of the doting age which is here in *CA* the reason for *Amans*' dismissal from Venus' court. Ll. 40–41 of Chaucer's *Envoy a Scogan* read like an allusion to this counsel:

> While I was yong, I put hir forth in prees
> But al shal passe that men prose or ryme.

2955. Such a last will and testament would presumably be in the nature of a farewell to love as a theme for poetry. Gower may have had in mind Thomas Usk's *Testament of Love*. The phrase hardly implies, as some critics think, that Chaucer should produce a collection of love-stories. In the *Roman de la Rose* l'Amant's testament is simply 'To Bialacoil leve I myn hert / Al hool' (*Romaunt*, 4610 ff.).

The omission of this passage in the second recension does not necessarily indicate a change of the poet's feelings towards Chaucer: see Fisher, *John Gower*, pp. 119–20.

2957. *recorde*: 'bear witness to it', so as to make it (legally) binding.

2970. The Latin leonine verses in the full text at this point (Macaulay, ii. 468) allude to the occasion described in the Prologue of the first recension, when Gower met the king whilst being rowed across the Thames at flood tide:

> My liege lord par chaunce I mette;
> And so befel, as I cam nyh,
> Out of my bot, whan he me syh,
> He bad me come in to his barge.
> And whan I was with him at large,
> Amonges othre thinges seid
> He hath this charge upon me leid,
> And bad me doo my besynesse
> That to his hihe worthinesse
> Some new thing I scholde boke
> That he himself it mihte loke
> After the forme of my writynge. (Prol. 42–53*)

2975. Following the traditional interpretation of Gen. i. 26 (*faciamus hominem*, etc.).

2991 ff. This was hardly true of the later years of Richard's reign. Langland too had enjoined the young king to mingle justice with mercy (*Piers Plowman*, Prol. B. 132 ff.).

3007 ff. Shakespeare was to use the same figure of the same King: *Richard II*, iii. iii. 62 ff.

3023. *of his heyh suffraunce*: 'by his kingly forbearance'.

3030. A doctrine elaborated in *Peace*: see below, p. 124.

3061-2. Cf. the Host's ideal of 'tales of best sentence and moost solaas' (*CT*, A. 798).

3064. In the second recension rhetoric is here associated with 'Tullius', i.e. Cicero, as in *CT*, F. 721-6: Cicero's *De Inventione* and the pseudo-Ciceronian *Rhetorica ad Herennium* being the chief sources for medieval rhetorical doctrine. In *CA*, vii, a survey of the seven arts, Rhetoric is divided into Grammar and Logic (vii. 1507-94); the discussion there is the first account of the art in English: cf. J. J. Murphy, *PQ*, xli (1962), pp. 401 ff. The disavowal of rhetoric in the present passage (cf. *HF*, 858-9, 1099-1100) is itself a rhetorical device expressive of auctorial humility (see E. R. Curtius, *European Literature* . . ., ed. cit., Exc. II) and examples of most other rhetorical figures can be found in Gower's work, though it is true that he eschews the more ornate 'forms of rhetoric'.

3074. For the personal reference in 'mi muse', cf. Chaucer's *Lenvoy a Scogan,* 38 ('Ne thynke I never of slep to wake my muse').

3086. Cf. the OF proverb 'Tant con li gens est biaus, tant le doint l'en lessier', and the allusions in *Romeo and Juliet*, I. iv. 39, v. 123.

3091. *dedly hele*: cf. the oxymorons with which Bk. i opened and the 'jolif wo' of vi. 84, etc.

3100. the second recension reads:

> Such love is goodly forto have,
> Such love mai the bodi save,
> Such love mai the soule amende,
> The hyhe god such love ous sende, etc.

3102. 'For it brings no retribution that can lie heavy on the conscience, but rather sets us free from a bad conscience and brings us reward in this life and in the life to come.'

Epistola. Since Chaucer links Gower and 'philosophical' Strode (*Tr*, v. 1857) it is tempting to suppose that Ralph Strode, sometime Fellow of Merton College, Oxford, is the author of these lines. The same writer contributed the commendatory lines attached to the *Vox Clamantis*, comparing Gower's triple achievement to Virgil's.

PEACE

From the poem addressed to Henry IV (Macaulay, **i,**
pp. 481–92, ll. 99–133)

The sentiments of the poem as a whole (it is 385 ll. long) are found elsewhere in Gower's works, notably in *CA*, iii. 2251–638, and *Mirour*, 125 ff. It reflects the feeling against the continuation of the French wars that grew in force at the turn of the century: cf. the poem by Charles d'Orleans printed by, e.g., B. Woledge in the *Penguin Book of French Verse* (1), p. 288, Hoccleve's *Regement of Princes* (EETS, ES, 72, 1897), p. 192.

121. 'whose faith thou hast partly to guide'.

382. *see the werre*: 'look to the war'.

383. The Great Schism was not yet ended.

BALADES

For notes on these balades (which in their sentiments much resemble Froissart's forty 'balades amoureuses' in various metres), see Macaulay, *Works*, vol. iii, and for comment on the two St. Valentine's Day balades see Bennett, *The Parlement of Foules*, pp. 138–9. Texts and translations of Balades I and II in Macaulay's edition are printed by Henry Morley, *English Writers*, vol. iv, and of nos. XXIV and XXXVII in B. Woledge (ed.), *The Penguin Book of French Verse* (1), pp. 230–2, where they may be ompared with contemporary French balades on the adjacent pages.

EXTRACTS FROM THE *MIROUR DE L'OMME*

i. *The marriage of Sin's daughters* (ll. 841–948)

The *Mirour* begins with an allegorical vision. Sin, born of the Devil, gives birth to Death, who engenders on her seven daughters, the Vices (an ancient motif). The Devil thereupon holds his 'parlement pour l'omme enginer' and Temptation is sent to entrap Man. Conscience and Reason frustrate this design, whereupon Sin consults with the World (le Siecle) who proposes marriage with each of the daughters in turn.

The account has obvious resemblances to that in *Paradise Lost*, Books I and II, but there is no evidence that Milton ever saw the sole MS. extant.

ii. *A prayer to the Virgin* (ll. 29905–45)

Gower sees man as dependent in the last resort on the intercession of the Lady of Pity, Mary, maiden and mother, and so concludes the poem with the narrative of her birth, life, death and assumption, followed by this prayer based upon her traditional names and attributes. It is incomplete as a few leaves are lost at the end of the MS.

(Passages illustrating other aspects of the poem, and showing Gower's interest in the commerce of his day will be found quoted or translated by Eileen Power in her *Medieval People* (Penguin ed., pp. 119, 140: see Index. See also M. W. Bloomfield, *The Seven Deadly Sins* (1952), pp. 194–5.)

PASSAGES FROM *VOX CLAMANTIS*★
i. (Book I. 783–816)

This extract is from an account of the Peasants' Revolt that was probably added after the first draft of the poem was completed. The description, for all its allegorical form, has the intensity of remembered experience. Men become beasts, and beasts run wild. London is pictured as the New Troy that became prey to the mob as the first Troy did to the Greeks. The narrator, like Aeneas, flees by ship—in this case, the ship of religion.

ii. (Book V. 735–86)

Book V is devoted to the duties and shortcomings of peasants, merchants, and craftsmen.

iii–v. (Book VII. 545–66; 637–60; 1289-1302)

In Book VII, c. 6, the proper purpose of man's creation is set forth, in preparation for a discourse on his present state. There are reminiscences here of Ovid's 'first man':

> Os homini sublimi dedit, caelumque videre
> iussit et erectos ad sidera tollere vultus.

(Met. i. 85–86)

★ [For notes on these passages see Macaulay's edition, and Stockton's translation in *The Complete Latin Works* (see p. xxi above): i, p. 67; ii, p. 213; iii, p. 266; iv, p. 464; v, p. 468.]

ADDENDA

VI (v. 4037 ff.) 'Juvente' = Juventa (Ovid). *fieldwode* is Gower's intention, on the basis of Ovid's *silva agresti*, and he is the first to use *vervain*: Ovid's *verbenis* apparently refers to laurel or similar twigs or boughs; *vervain* is *verbena officinalis*, 'formerly much valued for its medicinal properties' (*OED*).

puttes (4043), *pettes* (4047) are dialectal variants of *pittes*. For similar variants in Gower see K. Sisam, *Fourteenth Century Verse and Prose*, p. 249.

4049. *with honey meynd* ('mingled'). Ovid does not mention honey.

4054 represents *terrena numina civit* (*Met.* vii. 248). For *line* in the sense of 'series of persons' see *OED* s.v., 19 (where it is first cited from *Macbeth* IV. i. 117). In 4064 ff. *gone* = 'gasp', *spelling* = 'speaking', *cok* = cook, *rase* (4090) = 'run swiftly', *stede* (4096) = place, *laverock* (4100) = 'lark'; *strangeth* (4103) in the sense 'becomes strange or changed', is found only here.

4151. *medwe-grene* (cf. Ovid, *vernat humus*) is a unique ME instance of a compound only recorded by *OED* in a quotation dated 1794, when it is defined as 'lively green, in which however the yellow predominates'.

VII (v. 5670 n.). For further discussion of *tale and end* see Bennett and Smithers, *Early Middle English Verse and Prose*, pp. 306–7.

5923. *And bet it schal*: 'and it will be more fully avenged (*or*, punished) in the future' (since his shameful act (*defame*, 5925) will live in story).

VIII (viii. 2111–12 n.). The reference in *Ay.* must be to Seneca, Ep. 37: *si vis tibi omnia subjicere, subjice te rationi: multos reges, si ratio te rexerit.*

(viii. 2500). The translation offered in the note depends on the assumption that Gower has in mind some such reference as that inserted by Malory in his fifth book, c. 3 (*Works*, ed. Vinaver, p. 195): 'And sir Trystrams at that tyme beleft with Kynge Marke of Cornuayle for the love of La Beale Isode.' Yet the form of the past participle of the verb *ileve* would normally be *bileft* or *bileved*, not *believed*, as here. If Gower's form is construed as the pa. ptc. of *believe*, the sense must be 'accepted as lover by'.

GLOSSARY

When a word has a wide range of meanings those senses still current are not usually included in this glossary. An asterisk denotes words new or unique in form or meaning or otherwise of special lexical interest. Forms joined in MSS. (e.g. *tolite*) are not separated in this edition; but elision—except of *ne*—is generally marked by an apostrophe (e.g. *th'eir*). Except initially *y* is treated as *i*, and *u* sometimes as *w*.

abaissht, puzzled, startled; **for pure ~,** from sheer surprise.
abeie, abye, pay for; *pa. t.* **abohte.**
abide, wait, remain; *pr.* **abit,** *pa.* **abod.**
ablaste★, blew upon.
aboute, everywhere, round and round; **al ~,** throughout; **~ round,** round-about.
above, in a superior position; **ben ~,** be successful.
abreide, started, 'came to'.
achieved, finished, attained; **ben ~,** succeed, be successful (in gaining).
acord (*n.*), consent.
acorde (*v.*), agree; **acordant,** in agreement with, consonant with.
acquite, set free (from).
acroceth, gathers, gains.
adrad, afraid, in awe.
adresce, arrange, array.
af(f)aite, train, prepare; **~d,** controlled, governed (by): **evele ~d,** misshapen.
afflihte, was afflicted, disturbed.
affray, fear.
afire, (being) burnt.
after, according to.
age, old age.
agrise (*p.p.*), terrified.
al, (i) (*intensive*), quite, entirely; (ii) (*adj.*): **al this,** this entire; **al is in thee,** it is entirely in thy hands.
algate, in any case, assuredly.
alleide, accused.
allowe, approve, accept.
alongeth★, desires, longs.
als tyt, at once, forthwith.
also, as, just as.
alyhte, came down.

amendement, relief; **~ to syghen,** relief in sighing.
amiddes, in the middle of.
among, at times; **evere ~,** again and again.
amonte, signify, mean.
amorous, disposed to love, actuated by ideals of love.
amorwe, (on) the next day.
annuied, tired, weary.
anon, thereupon, at once.
any man, any one (at all).
apert, overt.
apointed, fixed, prescribed.
appalleth, makes anxious.
apparence, outward appearance.
appetit, desire (for).
appropred, dedicated, assigned.
aprise, learning, love, instruction.
aqueintance, companionship; **of ~,** in (female) company.
aquite (*v.*), clear.
ar, before, soon.
araied, prepared.
areche, succeed in reaching.
areste, delay, restrain.
arewe, arowe, in due order, succession.
ariste, rising; **sonne ~,** sunrise.
arms, (feats of) arms, weapons, armour.
art magique, occult science.
as of, as regards; **as in,** in; **as tho,** for the time being; **as who seith,** as if to say; **as he that,** like one who; **as ye that ben,** seeing that you are; **as be mi wit,** as far as I know; **as nought ne were,** as if nothing were amiss, had happened; **who as,** who so, if any . . .; **bot as,** except as.

as(s)ent, (*v.*) sent for; (*n.*) agreement, view.

aspie (*v.*), notice, see; (*n.*), watching; **upon ~,** under suspicious observation.

assay, (proven) quality; **assaies,** efforts.

assaied, examined, inspected.

assemble togedre, have intercourse.

assised, appointed.

assote, act foolishly; **~d of hir love so,** so infatuated by love for her.

assuage, leave off.

astat, estate, nature, condition, stages.

asterte, escape, avoid, prevent.

at, according to; **ate, atte,** at the.

atir, furnishing, requisites.

attached, taken prisoner, bound (by a writ).

atteinte, reached, got to.

attempre, restrain.

atwinne, in two; **part ~,** separate.

aunter, chance; **in ~ if,** on the chance that, in case.

avance, help by forwarding a marriage.

avantage, superiority; **caste his ~,** reckoned up the things in his favour.

aventure, chance; **bot as it falth in ~,** except fortune helps; **in ~,** in doubt, in balance; **stonde upon his ~,** take the consequences of his illhap. See also **per aventure.**

aventurous (knyht), knight errant.

avis, avys, judgement, opinion.

avise, learn, discover; (*refl.*) consider; **avised,** having deliberated; **ben ~,** take counsel, be guided.

avou, solemn undertaking.

awaite, watch (for), expect.

awake, keep awake.

aweie, gone past, over, 'no more'; **do ~,** put aside; **~ward,** aside, to the side; **mai no bet,** is powerless.

awhile (siththe), a short time ago.

awok, awoke, 'came to', roused (oneself).

axe, ask (for), examine (in confession).

axinge, question, inquiry.

ayein (*adv.*), back; **gon, come ~,** return; (*prep.*) towards; **~ the sonne,** in the sunlight; **~ ward,** round, towards, once again, in return.

ayer, in the year.

balance, scales; **in ~,** unstable, subject to change.

baldemoine, (root or leaf of) gentian.

banne (*v.*) curse.

bargain, undertaking.

barm, bosom.

bass, low.

be so, provided that.

be, by; **~feintise,** falsely.

be that, since.

beau retret*, seemly withdrawal.

becam (wher he), what became of him.

beclipte, embraced.

beginne, enter into.

bego, work upon, furnish; **begon,** covered, loaded, adorned.

begonne (*p.p.*), come upon.

beheste, promise(s).

behiete, behote (*v.*), promise, warrant; *pa. t.* **behihte.**

beholde, bound in duty.

beknowe, acknowledge(d), confess(ed).

beleve, remain, linger.

believed*, accepted as a lover.

belongeth, appertains, befits.

bemene (*v.*), pity.

ben, are.

benyce*, make a fool of oneself.

beschaded, overshadowed, shaded.

beseie, besein, furnished, dressed, disposed; **wo ~,** sad-looking.

besette, employ.

besien, busy, occupy (oneself).

besinesse, activity, occupation; **do ~,** apply, devote (oneself).

besischipe, effort, exertion.

beste (to the), in the best possible way.

beste, beastlike, loathsome, creature.

betake, commend; (*p.p.*) assigned, allotted.

betauhte, delivered.

bethoghte (*refl.*), considered, realised; **wel bethoght,** well advised; **ben ~,** to meditate; be disposed.

betid, befallen, come to pass.

bewaked*, passed without sleep.

bewhaped, bewildered, confused.

bewelde (*refl.*), control, take care of (oneself).

bidde, ask (for), pray, command; *pa. t.,* **bad, bod,** *pl., p.p., pa. sjv.,* **bede.**

bille, petition.

bime, for me, in my company.

blame, censure, criticism.

blente, obscured, concealed.

blind(e), blind(ed), dull, deficient, confused.

(as) blyve, as soon as possible, at once.

boiste, buiste, box, jar.

bold, confident, certain; **made him ∼** (upon), gained the confidence (of).

bombard, a double reed instrument, the bass shawm.

bot, unless, except for, save that; **∼ as,** save as; **∼ if,** unless; **ne ∼,** only.

bote, relief, remedy; **do ∼,** give relief.

bouele, intestine.

bowe, bow, submit.

bowh, branch(es).

brak, broke (up).

brede, breadth; **in ∼ and lengthe,** fully, in all parts.

brid, bird.

bringe (in), entrap.

brod(e), breadth; **on daies** (*g.*) **∼,** in broad daylight.

buile(n), boil.

buiste, boiste, box.

caitif, wretch.

can, conne, know (how to), be able to; *pa. t.* **couthe, cowthe.**

canele, cinnamon.

capitain, castellan.

care, misery, anxiety, pain (of love).

carecte, charm.

carole, round dance accpd. by singing.

carte, chariot.

cas, event, plight.

cast, throw of dice; **ate laste ∼,** at one's last throw.

caste, turn, reflect, notice, fore-ordain; **∼ chance on dees,** try one's luck at dice.

cauhte (*p.p.* **cauwht**), took, conceived, felt, experienced.

cause, occasion, condition, (legal) case, reason, matter.

cercle, orbit, course (of a heavenly body) ;ecliptic o fthe sun.

certein, (*a.*) fixed, definite, true; (**as** *n.*), assurance.

certeinete, trust, reliance.

certes, indeed.

cha(u)nce, opportunity, occasion, luck, lot, happening, fate, one's fortune as predicted by the fall of dice; **til the ∼ falle,** until the number turns up; **upon ∼,** by chance.

char, carriage, chariot.

charge, interest, concern, attention, offspring.

charke, creak.

chaumberere, lady in waiting, maid-servant.

chele, cold(ness).

ch(i)ere, face, countenance, expression, behaviour; **do, make ∼,** treat kindly, hospitably, humour; **tok ∼ in honde,** became cheerful, took heart.

chese, choose (*imper.* ches).

chitre, jabber.

chivalerous, full of knightly spirit.

Chymerie, Cimmeria (land of darkness).

citole, kind of zither.

Cizile, Sicily.

clepe, call, call out to.

clerk, cleric.

cles, claws.

client*, subject, follower, servant.

clippe, (i) embrace, (ii) cut.

clos, (*n.*) seclusion, hiding; (*adj.*) secluded, hidden.

coise, (*lit.* rump?) hag.

collacioun, discourse, reflexion.

compaignie, fellowship, intimacy; put out of **∼,** exclude.

compasse, contrive, do, undertake, take in.

compleigne, make complaint over, lament.

complexioun, disposition, character (as produced by a predominant 'humour').

compteth, considers, sets (at); **∼ at noght,** considers worthless.

comun (*adj.*) customary; **my ∼ us,** usually.

comune (*n.*), fellowship, company.

com(m)une, (v.) associate, communicate; ~ of, to confer, talk about.
concluded, frustrated, contradicted, given a final answer; ben ~, be in agreement, be determined.
conclusio(u)n, end; of ~, finally, in the end.
condicioun, nature, quality.
conforme (refl.), adapt.
congeide★, dismissed.
conjure, incantation, magic.
conseil, council, counsel, advice; prive ~, secret ~; ben ~, to be a secret; for no ~, despite all urging; hiden ~, keep a secret.
conspired★, sighed after, craved for: cf. G's conspirement★.
constellacion, horoscope (position of a planet in relation to the ascendant sign of the zodiac).
cont(i)enaunce, appearance, looks; piken mi ~, cast my glance.
contourbed, perturbed, distressed.
contretaile, retribution.
convey, guide, lead.
cope, cloak, mantle.
corage, heart.
cornemuse, hornpipe (a form of bagpipe).
cote, tunic, kirtle.
courbe, bent, twisted.
cours, course, process, way.
cousinage, kinship, consanguinity; stod of ~ to, was kin to.
couthe, see can.
covenant, promise, assurance.
covert (in), (in) secrecy.
coverture, stealth.
covine, agreement.
craft, skill; ~eliche, skilfully.
crye, beg for.
cure, (1) remedy, care; (2) custody, authority; (3) court, kingdom; worldes ~, worldly, temporal business.
curious, careful, inquisitive, much exercised.
curteis, gracious, considerate, kind.

dai, day; thi daies ende, the end of the time appointed; be ~es olde, in days gone by, see also brod.

dar, dare; pr. sjv. dore.
da(u)nger, resistance, disdain; withoute ~, without reserve, freely.
daunte, subdue, overpower.
debat, dispute; stant upon ~, be uncertain, unpredictable.
debonaire, quiet-mannered, kindly, gracious.
deceipte, trickery; in ~ of, in order to deceive.
dede (i), deed; in ~, actually.
dede (ii), dead (man); deep; ~ly, fatal.
deduit, delight, pleasure.
dees, dice.
defalte, defect.
defende, forbid.
degre(e), state, fashion; riht in such ~, exactly in the same way; be degres, in due order.
delice, delight.
delit, of ~, delightedly.
delivere★, to tell.
deme, judge, pronounce judgement; (imp. demeth).
departed, parti-coloured.
dere, (v.), harm; (adv.), dearly.
descende, come down (fig.).
descharge, benefit, relief from misfortune.
desclosed★, viewed.
descorde, differ, act differently.
deserve, earn, win.
desese(d), suffering, ill: see disese.
de(s)face, disfigure, mar.
deslaied★, delayed.
despeired★, stormy (of weather), unfavourable.
despente, spent, passed, occupied.
desputeison, controversy, debate.
destourbe, destroy, trouble.
devise, plan, describe, relate.
devocioun, devout practice, desire (to do something); with ~, devoutly.
disese, discomfort, trouble, suffering, cause of affliction.
disport, desport, pleasant aspect, 'lighter side'.
dispocioun, constitution, nature.
distance, discord; fellen in ~, fell into disagreement.
do, cause; ~ the lawe, observe the practice; (pa. t.) dede upon, put on.

dom, judgement.

doute, fear.

dradde, dredde, was afraid of; ~ **hym of his harmes,** was worried about mishaps that might befall him.

drawe, draw out; *pa. t.* **drogh, drowh,** moved, proceeded. ~ **hir adryh,** withdrew (to a safe distance); **of** ~, take off.

dreche, torment, ~ **forth,** while away.

dreinte, drowned.

dryhe, endure.

duelle, linger.

eft, next, then.

ek, also.

elles, otherwise.

em, uncle.

emprise, undertaking, design.

enbrouded, decorated, embroidered.

enbrouderie*, embroidery.

encluyed, crippled by a nail in a hoof.

ende, conclusion; what is to be done; **at thi daies** ~, at your time limit.

enderday (this), the other day.

enforme, instruct, guide.

ensample, example.

enspired, breathed into.

entaille, fashion.

entamed, laid open; **newe** ~, resumed.

entendance, service.

entendant, attentive.

entendement, understanding.

entente, will, desire, meaning, purpose; **with hole** ~, wholeheartedly, completely; **to that** ~, for that purpose.

enterement, funeral, memorial service.

entriketh, deceives.

er, before; ~ **this,** up to the moment.

eschuie, succeed in avoiding, escape (something ordained).

ese, relief, comfort; **wel at** ~, wholly at peace; **be** ~, easily.

esmaie, (*refl.*) frighten, disconcert; **esmaied,** timid.

espleit, success.

espo(u)saile, marriage or betrothal.

essoine, excuse.

evene (*n.*), equal, match; agreement; **setten al in** ~, compose, balance.

evene (*adv.*), equally.

evere, continually, always; ~ **in on,** continually.

evidence, sign, example; **in** ~, as an illustration.

everychar, each and every one.

everydiel, fully, in every detail.

excluded, prevented.

excused, let off, passed over; disguised, counteracted.

expresse, explicit.

fade, pale, discoloured, feeble, wasted.

faie, magical; (*as sb.*) being of magical power.

faire, graciously, courteously.

faiterie, deceit, false pretences.

faitours, deceivers, hypocrites.

falle, befall, happen, arise; **felle upon the chance,** came to the point, situation; *see also,* **chance, foule.**

fame, renown, repute, report.

fare (*n.*), condition (*v.*), fare, walk, go; *pa. t.* **ferde.**

fees, wages; tenure in an office of feudal service; estate.

feigne, (1) dissimulate, make pretence; (2) produce, bring about.

felaschipe, company; **don** ~, keep company.

fele, many.

fell(it), (it) happened (*w. dat.*).

felonie, wickedness, crime.

ferforth, far.

feste, feast, enjoyable occasion, event; **maken** ~, make merry.

fette, fetch, take; *p.p.* **fet.**

fiele, think, experience. **to** ~, feeling.

figure, image, likeness.

fille, abundance, heart's desire.

flietende, floating.

flor, ground.

flour, virginity.

fond, found.

fonde, (*tr.*) experience, discover; (*intr.*) endeavour.

for, because, since.

forbere, relinquish, go without.

forfare(n), destroyed; **a man** ~, one at the end of his tether, a castaway.

forlith, seduces, rapes; **forlein** (*p.p.*) lain with, had illicit relations with.

forlore, utterly lost.

forme, pattern; **upon the ~,** following the established mode, ritual.

forsake, deny, ignore, renounce; (*p.p.*) omitted; **~ with,** deserted by.

forschop, transformed into something ugly; *p.p.* **forschape.**

forth, on, forward; **teche it ~,** spread it around; **~ with,** (i) together with; (ii) at once; **forth with that,** thereupon.

forthi, wherefore, therefore.

for(to), (in order) (to); **forto preise** (*etc.*), to be praised, praiseworthy (*etc.*); **forto speke of,** as regards.

fortune (*n.*), luck, fortune(s); (sometime personified).

fortune (*v.*), control, bring about, cause, destine.

foryete, forget; *pa. t.* **foryat.**

foryift, forgiveness.

foul, ugly; **foule,** badly; **~ him falle,** ill may it fare with him.

fro, (away) from; **~ when,** whence.

front, forehead.

frounceth, wrinkles.

fulfille, accomplish.

furgh, strip.

game, pleasure, festivity, revelry; action, undertaking.

gan, began; *with inf.,* did.

gate, way.

gaudes, large ornamental beads in a rosary.

gentilesse, nobility of birth, rank, character or manners.

gentle, of noble birth or character; courteous.

gete, take hold on, recover.

go, walk, be alive; *p.p.,* gone, departed this life; **~ upon hir hond,** be in her company **~ beside,** am slighted.

good, wealth, property; **this worldes good,** the wealth of this world.

goodly, (*adj.*) pleasant; (*adv.*) graciously, pleasantly.

gore, gown; **gile under ~,** concealed treachery.

grace, favour, goodness, virtue, mercy.

grant, accord, consent.

grantdame, grandmother.

grant merci, thanks.

gre(e)ne, young, immature, recent, bitter, painful.

Gregeis, Greek(s).

grevance, grief, annoyance, sorrow.

greves, groves.

guye, lead, control; **for to ~,** in his keeping.

halsen, interpret.

halt, holds, observes, follows; *pa. t.* **hielde,** kept (*sts. refl.*); *see* **holde.**

haltede, went haltingly, lame.

halvinge, half, in part.

hap(p), happening.

haste (his time), speed (his enterprise).

hastihiede*, haste; **in ~,** speedily.

he which, the man who; **as he that,** like a man who (sts. otiose).

hebenus, ivory.

hed,[^chief; **tofor myn ~** in front of me.

hele (*n.*), health, cure, restoration, salvation, profit; (*v.*) cover.; *p.p.* **heled.**

hell, hull, hill; **helle,** of hell.

hem, here, them, their.

hente, seize; *pa. t.* took, drew, snatched; *p.p.* **hent.**

hep, host, quantity.

herte rote, bottom of the heart.

heste, command(ment).

heved, hefd, head.

hevy, sad.

hevynesse, sorrow.

hiede, heed; **good ~ on hire he tok,** he observed her (so) narrowly; **~ nam,** took heed, fully realized.

hiele, heel.

hiere, hear (of), listen (to).

hihte, was called.

ho(ther), 'enough!'

holde (*adj.*), beholden, obliged; **~ of,** bound by; (*n.*), stronghold.

holde for, honour, regard as.

hol(e), entire, whole, cured, healthy.

hond, hand; **of his ~,** as regards valour in fight; **out of honde,** away; **hath on ~,** has to bear, suffer; **take on ~,** undertake, wager, apply osf. to; **put hire ~,** put out her hand, made a gesture; **in ~,** in pledge.

honeste, proper, honourable.

hongeth, hangs, is on the subject of.

hore, hoary.

hors, horse(s) (*g. pl.* horse; ~ knave, groom).

hote, called, named.

hove, hover, heave to, sit reined in.

hovedance*, lively court dance.

how so, although.

hyngen (*pa. pl.*), hung.

if (that), if; bot if, unless.

ilke, selfsame.

impresse*, fix (eye).

infortune, evil fortune.

insihte, perception, awareness.

it, something, one thing; how that it is, how things stand; as it were (*sts.*), as if I were.

janglinge, quarrelling, discord.

jape, trick, delusion.

jargoun (*n.*), twittering; (*v.*), twitter.

jolif, joyous, gay.

juise, judgement, punishment.

jus, juice.

kempde, combed.

kep, heed; tok ~, was aware, attended.

kepe (*pa. t.* kepte), guard, wait for, care (for); to kepe, in (my) keeping.

kertle, gown.

keste, kissed.

kid, known, revealed.

kinde, species, manner, race; Nature; in ~, naturally.

knette, knit, splice.

knowe (*pa. t.* knew), know (of), understand, recognize.

knowlechinge, knowledge, acquaintance.

lacke, lak, want, fault.

ladde (*p.p.*), guided, moved.

ladi (*g.*), lady's; ~hede*, ladyship.

ladischipe, rank, quality, superior position of a lady.

lancegay, kind of lance.

lapped, wrapped, folded.

large (at), without restraint.

lasse, less; ever leng the ~, the longer [I try] the less [I learn].

lassed, made less.

laste (ate, to the), in the upshot,

finally, as conclusion, to its end; to my ~, finally.

launde, glade.

lawe, custom; do the ~, observe the custom, correct procedure.

left, left (out); ~ bihinde, left out.

leyhe, (*v.*), laugh, smile.

leisir, opportunity.

lere (*n.*), loss; schape to the ~, destined to lose his life; (*v.*), learn, teach.

lese, lose, *3rd sg. pr.* lest, *p.p.* lore.

lest (*imp.*), it pleases; *cf.* list.

lest (*imper.*), listen.

leste (ate), (at) least.

lete, leave (off); ~ aweie, let pass, ignore; let, *pa. t.* caused, thought; *p.p.* left alone.

lette (*n.*), hindrance, delay.

lette (*v.*), prevent, hinder; (*p.p.*) let.

leve, stay; leave (behind), hold off, let go.

l(i)evere, sooner (comp. of lief); *sup.* lievest, most willingly.

liche, alike.

lief, dear, pleasant.

lien, restraining bond.

liered (*p.p.* of lere), told.

lieve, trust, believe.

lif, living being, person.

ligance, allegiance.

ligge, lie.

lihtly, lightly, easily.

likende, likinge, pleasing.

liketh (*imp.*), (it) pleases; *pr. sjv.* like.

likynge, pleasure.

linde, (lime) tree.

list (*imp.*), please, want; *pa. t.* list(e): me list nothing, I in no way desire.

lite, little; ne bot a ~, only a little.

lith (*n.*), limb, feature; (*v.*), lies.

loenge, praise.

loketh, looks; ~ forth, peers; ~ about, keep watch; (*imper.*) loke, see; ~ how, make sure that.

longe and late, after a long delay.

longeth, pertains.

lordschipe*, a lord's protection.

lore, teaching; toke hem into ~, undertook their instruction.

lost, loss.

lothe, be hateful (to).

loure, lower, frown.

loute, bow, make obeisance.

loweth, humbles.

lowh, laughed.

lucre, gain, profit.

lust, pleasure, desire; (*pl.*) attractions, pleasing qualities; **set him in his ~ above,** give him success.

lusti, pleasant, pleasing, vigorous.

madle, male.

mai, can (do), will, intend, avail; *pa. t.* **mihte; mochel~,** had great strength.

maide, virgin.

make (*n.*), mate.

make (*v.*), (i) cause, bring about; (ii) compose verses; *pa. t. pl.* **maden;** *p.p.* **mad.**

malencolie, sudden violent anger.

malencolien, addicted to sudden anger.

malgre, despite; **~ hem,** despite themselves.

manace, threat(s), prophecy of evil outcome; **maken ~,** show hostile intent.

manere, good manners, breeding; **whom lacketh no ~,** who is of excellent manners.

manneskinde, human nature.

marches (*n.*), borderlands.

marche (*v.*), border.

matiere, subject, concern, state.

may, maiden.

mede, meed, reward; **~ful,** meritorious.

medicine, cure.

medleth, mix, mingle.

meknesse, gentleness, compassion.

memoire, recollection, remembrance.

men, men, people; 'one'.

me(e)ne, mean, imply, involve, speak.

merthes, delights, rejoicing.

meschief, evil, harm.

message, errand.

mesure, proportion, limit; **tempre the ~,** observe due proportion (in).

mete, food, bait.

meette, mete, dream; *pa. t.* **mette.**

mirre, myrrh.

misdede, acted wrongly.

misse, fail.

mistime, do, perform, say at a wrong time, in wrong order.

moche, many (a).

mochel, muchel, great (no. of).

mod, mood, mind, disposition.

molde (i), fashion; (ii), earth.

mone, be the, by moonlight.

more, blackamoor.

mot(e), must, may; *pa. t.* **moste.**

mowe, may.

muse, reflect, gaze.

musette*, a kind of bagpipe.

mynde, memory, remembrance.

nacion, class; **gentil ~,** folk of gentle birth and breeding.

name, reputation, common talk; **eschuie a ~,** escape the repute.

namely, nameliche, in particular.

nargh, narrow.

natheles, nevertheless, moreover.

ne, not, nor; **~ bot,** only.

nede, necessity; **upon the ~,** in a time of need.

nede(s), nedly (*adv.*), of necessity.

nedeth (*imp.*), it is necessary.

nerr(e), nearer.

neyhe (*v.*), approach, get near.

newe, anew.

noise, make a noise.

nom, nam, took; **~ good hiede,** watched carefully; cf. **hiede.**

noman, no one, nobody.

norrice, nurse, nourisher.

not (= **ne wot**), know(s) not.

nothing, not at all, not in the least.

nother, neither.

novellerie*, novelty.

nyce, foolish; **~te,** folly.

o, a, one.

occupacion, calling, activity.

of (i), about, concerning, by, with, for, in, from; **of that,** from what, because, since; (ii), off.

office, office, function.

ofte sithes, many times, often.

oght, anything.

on, one; **~ and ~,** one by one; **one,** single.

onde, breath.

oppose, ask questions.

opposit*, opposite aspect (*astron.*: *see OED,* s.v. *opposition* 3).

or . . . or, either . . . or.

ordeine, determine, settle, prescribe.

ordre, office, rank.
othergate, otherwise.
otherwhile, sometimes.
othre, other things.
oultrage, deed of violence.
out(e) quite, abroad; **telle ~,** speak out; **~ of reule / the wei,** beyond limit or control; **~ward,** abroad; **~with,** on the outside.
over, over and above; **~ this,** further; **~ more,** moreover.
overal, everywhere, throughout.
overpasse, pass by, away, over; avoid, let go.
overrunne, run over, run out.
overseie★, overseen, deceived, rash.
overspradde, covered.

pai(e)d (of), pleased (with).
paramour, lover.
parconner, partner.
parlement, council, assembly.
passage, voyage, departure.
passe(over), surpass.
peine, pain, distress; **do thi ~,** endeavour.
peinte, embellish with rhetoric.
pelrinage, pilgrimage.
per aventure, per cas, perhaps, by chance.
pernable, proper to be taken.
perrie, precious stones, jewellery.
pie, magpie.
piece, at every, completely.
plat, flat, downright.
plein, (*adj.*) plain, simple, straightforward; (*adv.*) fully, plainly.
pleine, complain.
pleinliche, pleinly, plainly, straightforwardly: with decision.
plesance, pleasure; **do the ~,** perform the pleasing duty.
plesant, pleasing.
plie, submit.
plit, state of things, manner.
plowh, plough (land).
point, manner, condition, item, matter, detail, decision; **in such ~,** thus, finally; **fro ~ to ~,** in every particular, in detail.
porpos, resolve; **no ~ take,** do nothing decisive.

port★, bearing, purport.
positif, formal, enacted.
p(o)urchace, obtain, acquire.
practique, moral science.
preche, warn, admonish.
preid, submitted.
pres(s), crowd; **in presse,** down below.
presence, royal state, attendance.
pride, magnificent ornamentation.
prie, peer at, observe.
pris, prize, reward, excellency; **of ~,** worthy, excellent.
prive, private, secret, trusted, belonging to a private circle.
privete, privite, secrecy, a thing kept secret.
prolificacion, fruitfulness.
propre, due, regular; **~te,** nature.

qued, evil (thing), harm, villain.
queinte, elaborate; **make it ~,** act artfully, refine upon it.
queintised★, adorned.
queynte, quenched; *p.p.* **queynt.**
querele, (cause of) complaint (at law); hostility.
quit, let off.
quod, said.
qwok, shook.

rage (*n.*), fury, violent sexual desire.
rage (*v.*), behave amorously.
rather, sooner; **rathest,** soonest.
ravine, act of rapine.
real, royal.
reclamed, tamed, subdued.
record (*n.*), written record; **of ~,** in writing, as far as was known.
recorde (*v.*), ponder, remember, bear in mind, relate.
recoverir, remedy, expedient.
reddour, harshness.
red(e) (*n.*), counsel, plan; **what is to ~,** what is advisable; **sette ~, devise** a plan.
rede (*v.*), advise, deliberate.
reformed, changed back to **one's** proper shape.
refte, removed.
reherce, repeat, utter.
reles, act of freeing; **plein ~, full** discharge.

relieved, freed, assisted, lightened of care.

remembrance, memory, mention; **take ~,** bear in mind.

remenaunt, remainder, other things pertaining; **of al the ~,** as to the rest.

remene, relate, apply by way of illustration.

remue, (re-)move.

renomee, renown.

rente, revenue.

repentaile, repentance.

respite, delay.

reste, (place of) peace, freedom from distress.

retenue, service, **make his ~,** take service with.

reule, principle, norm, discipline, order; **out of ~,** in an irregular, disordered state.

reverence, deference; **for whos ~,** out of deference to whom; **at ~,** on account (of).

rewe, have pity; **forto ~,** pitiable.

riht (*adv.*), very, exactly.

rihte (*adj.*), proper, true, correct, direct.

rihtes, (at alle), at all points, in every respect.

riote, revelry, wantonness.

rivele, be wrinkled.

rode, a ride, journey on horseback.

route (*n.*), troop; **route** (*v.*), snore.

rowthe, matter of sorrow.

rucke, crouch.

ruide, violent, ungentle.

same, together.

Sarazines, infidels.

sauf, safe; **~ly,** safely.

save, safe, intact, free from danger, unlikely to cause harm.

sawe, discourse, tale.

schal, is to, must (be); *pa. t.* **scholde.**

schallemele, shawm (kind of oboe).

schape, contrive, bring about, appoint, prepare, devise, agree; *pa. t.* **schop.**

schawe, wood.

scherte, undergarment.

schewe (*imper.*), tell, make known, explain.

scheweth (*refl.*), appears.

schode, divide.

scole, school, company, profession; doctrine, lore.

seal(es), under ~ write, in writing confirmed by seal.

seewolf, voracious sea-fish.

sekerliche, assuredly.

selk, silk.

selve, very, selfsame.

se(n), on to ~, to behold; **~ out,** discern; **godd hire se,** God protect her.

sene, plain, visible.

sentence, meaning.

sett, although.

sette, lay down, establish, place, settle, attack, commit, resolve, take account; **~ behinde,** postpone; *pr. t. and p.p.* **set.**

sewe, pottage.

sey(forth), tell (on).

sielde (whanne), seldom.

sih(e), saw.

signet, small seal (as set in ring).

sike (*v.*), sigh.

sikernesse, assurance, pledge; **for ~ of mariage,** to make the marriage binding.

silogime, specious, subtle argument.

simple, humble, plain; **~ of port,** humble in bearing, demeanour.

sist, sittest; **siete,** *pa. t. pl.* sat.

sit(te), befits.

sithe(s), time(s).

sithen, siththe, since, ago; **ofte ~,** often; **~ go noght longe,** not long ago since.

skile (*n.*), reason, statement by way of argument; (*v.*), reason.

sky, cloud.

slee, slay.

slepi, inducing sleep.

slow, sluggish.

sly, cunning; *sup.* **slyheste.**

smal, slender.

so as, even as, since, insofar as.

softe, gently, quietly.

somdel, somewhat.

somerfare, state, array, of summer.

sonde, message, warning, intimation.

sone (*n.*), grandson.

sone (*adv.*), at once, forthwith.

sor, wound; **sore,** sorely, much.
sotie, folly.
soune, utter.
space, leisure, opportunity.
(in)special, in detail, specifically, in a distinctive way.
sped, success, prosperity.
spedde, succeeded.
sp(i)eke, spoke; **spekynges,** discourse.
spille, perish; destroy, waste.
sporne, strike, stumble (on or against).
stage, degree; **the hihe ∼,** the high places (homes of the gods).
stant, stands, is, remains, exists; **it ∼ of,** this is the case as regards; (*pl.*). **stonde,** are established; *pa. t.* **stod.**
st(i)ere, guide, move.
sterte(n), sprang.
sterve, die.
stile, character, characteristic manner.
stille, keep silence.
stounde, time.
sto(c)k, log; **∼ overthrowe,** dead log.
straghte, strawhte, made one's way.
strange (*adj.*), unfamiliar; **∼ to,** unacquainted with, hostile to.
strange (*v.*), alienate; grudge.
strawht, straightway.
stre, straw.
streite, closely, directly.
strengthe, force, validity.
styh, mounted.
such(e), of like kind; **∼ on,** a certain person.
sufficance, ability.
suffise, be able, competent, capable of.
suie, follow, conform to; **suiende,** following.
suite, garb, dress; **of o ∼,** clothed in the same garb or colour.
suore (*p.p.*), sworn (to secrecy).
suppose, imagine, conjecture.
swerve, turn.
swerth, swears.
swevene, dream.
swote, sweet(-smelling), pleasant.

take, give, seize, take (as husband); **∼ in mynde,** recall; **∼ hir nyh,** embrace; **∼ ensample,** follow the example; *pa. t.* **tok.**
tale (*n.*), speech; **tale(n)** (*v.*), speak.

tarie, delay, put off.
taxe, task, engagement, undertaking.
teche, tell, guide, impart: **∼ it forth,** make it known; **∼yng,** instruction.
telle, speak, name in order.
tempre, moderate, restrain, mingle, tune.
tene, trouble.
than(ne), then.
thar, ought, have occasion to.
thenke, (i) resolve, intend, (ii) *imp.* seem; *pa. t.* **thoghte.**
ther(as), where; **∼ is many of yow,** many of you are . . .; **∼ ayein,** opposed to that; **∼ to,** moreover, needful.
thewed (wel), well instructed, well conducted, of good qualities.
thilke (the ilke), that same.
thing, matter, concern, creature, event, fact, property, 'something'.
tho (*adv.*), then; (*pron.*) those.
thonk, thanks, gratitude, favour, goodwill; **∼ deserve,** earn favour.
thrinne, therein.
throwe, time.
thurgh, all over; **∼ soght,** searched; **∼ nome,** pierced, penetrated.
tide, time.
tih, tyh, went.
til whanne, until.
time(s), favourable occasion.
tymliche, betimes, soon.
tirant (as *adj.*), tyrannous, cruel.
tobreke, break, tear, to pieces; (*p.p.*) **tobroke.**
tofore, before, in front.
tolite, too little.
torne about, revolve.
tosprad, spread [over shoulders].
totore, torn to pieces.
touche, is related; **∼ of,** treat of, touch on; **∼ ende of,** concerning, with regard to.
toward, inclined, favourable, to.
treten (upon), treat (of), deal (with).
travail, journey(ing).
travaile, strive: *refl.*, put osf. to the trouble.
travers, disadvantage, obstacle.
triste (*v.*), trust; **forto ∼,** trustworthy.
trouble, discoloured, muddy.

trowthe, truth, fidelity, assurance; ~ **beere,** remained faithful.
truffles, trifles.
trusse, carry in a pack.
tweie, two.
tye, case.

unavised, unwise(ly).
unbehovely, unsuitable, unfit.
uncouth*, unrecognizable.
underfonge, receive, admit, accept.
unethes, scarcely.
ungladest, causest distress to.
unhappy, unfortunate, bringing disaster.
unmerciable, unmerciful, merciless.
unschette, open.
unsely, unhappy.
untame, wild.
untreuly, faithlessly.
untrewe, unfaithful, dishonest.
untrowthe, falsity, infidelity.
up, upon; ~ **alofte,** up.
uplefte, raised.
upon, on, into, with regard to, by reason of; **wakende ~ his lust,** alert, eager, to take its delight; ~ **astronomie,** according to the science of astronomy; **come ~,** happened to.
us (*n*.), practice.
use (*v*.), practise.

vecke, (ugly) old woman.
vengement, vengeance.
verray, due, proper.
vertu, efficacy.
vois, rumour, vote.

waf, wove.
wakere, one who rouses, stirs up another.
wanhope, (cause of) despair, hopelessness.
wantounesse*, capriciousness.
war, aware (of).
warant, pledge, security.
warie (*v*.), curse.
wawe, wave.
wedd, pledge, promise: **leith to ~,** pledges; **lith to ~,** lies in pawn.

weie, road; **in the ~,** 'as I go about'; **out of the ~,** 'out of rule', not subject to measure.
wel, fully, much; ~ **is,** it is well; ~ **farende,** good-looking; (*adj*.) happy.
wele, happiness, good fortune.
welked, withered.
welle, fountainhead, spring.
wende, thought, imagined.
went, turns, revolves; I *pr. sg.* **wende.**
werk, deeds.
what, (i) thing; (ii) whatever, who.
wher, whether, **-wher (that),** where; **wher as evere,** wheresoever.
whether, whichever.
whilom, formerly.
who, whoever, (if) anyone.
wif, woman.
wifles, unmarried.
wiht, creature, person; **worldes ~,** living creature; **no ~,** no-one.
will (*n*.), will, desire.
wik, wish, require; *pa. t.* **wolde,** wished, was anxious.
winne, gain, succeed in bringing to.
winter, year(s).
wise, (i) manner; **the same ~,** in the same way, manner; (ii) wise man.
(also)wiss, as surely as.
wissh, washed (*pl.* **wisshen**).
wite (*v*.), know, have any idea of, find out: (*pl*.), **witen:** *pa. t.* **wiste.**
wit(t), intelligence, wits.
withdrawe, reft away.
withholde, retained in service (by).
withoute, outside, left out.
withouten more, without more ado.
withstod, halted; *p.p.* **~stonde,** opposed.
wo, distress, pain, ill-fortune, sad fate.
wod(e), raging, furious, mad.
wole, wants (to), wishes (to): (*pa. t*.) **wolde.**
wollesak, sack of wool.
wommanhiede, womanliness.
wommanysch, resembling a woman.
wonder, wonderful.
wone (*n*.), custom; **of comune ~,** in accordance with usual custom.
wone (*v*.), dwell.

world, fortune, state, (condition in) life; **~es womman,** a woman like other women.

worschipe, honour, credit; **take ~ of,** get honour from.

(to the) worste, for the worse.

wreche, vengeance; **do ~,** take vengeance.

wreke, avenge; *pa. t.* **wroke.**

write, *p.p.* written.

wyssh, var. of *wissh.*

wyte (*n.*), blame; (*v.*) **to wyte,** to be blamed.

yare*, ready; answering readily to the helm.

yelpe (*refl.*), boast.

yhe, eye(s).

yive, give; **~ God a yifte,** vow to God; *pa. t.* **yaf** (*imper.* **yif**).

ymagerie, representation, pictures.

yolde, given back, restored.

yongly, youthful (in appearance).

PRINTED IN GREAT BRITAIN
AT THE UNIVERSITY PRESS, OXFORD
BY VIVIAN RIDLER
PRINTER TO THE UNIVERSITY